PRAISE FOR DANNY SEO AND
GENERATION REACT

"*Generation React*, the best how-to guide available for young people wanting to change the world, shows us that taking positive action is fun, easy, and something anyone can do—*today*. This book gives us all more hope for the future."

> —Sev Williams
> Executive Director of YES! (Youth
> for Environmental Sanity)

"Danny Seo's vision can inspire young people to act for a better world, and his practical guidance shows how to begin and how to succeed. The world is a far better place with Danny Seo's brand of social activism in it."

> —Neal D. Barnard
> President of the Physicians Committee
> for Responsible Medicine

"What a great book! Every parent concerned with building a better world should buy *Generation React* to turn his or her kids into citizen activists."

> —Michael Kieschnick
> President of Working Assets

"*Generation React* is truly a remarkable book. I have been an animal rights activist for more than thirty years and it served as an invaluable refresher course even for me."

> —Gretchen Wyler
> Founder and President of The Ark Trust

"We work with hundreds of 'Giraffes'—people who are sticking their necks out for the common good. Even in that outstanding company, Danny Seo stands out. His savvy and drive are all here in *Generation React*. It shows a new generation how to participate fully in a democracy that sorely needs the energy, concern, and smarts that Seo has put in these pages."

—Ann Medlock
President of The Giraffe Project

GENERATION REACT

ACTIVISM FOR BEGINNERS

DANNY SEO

Ballantine Books • New York

http://www.randomhouse.com

LIBRARY OF CONGRESS CATALOGING-IN-PUBLICATION DATA
Seo, Danny.
    Generation react : activism for beginners / Danny Seo.—1st ed.
      p.   cm.
    Includes index.
    ISBN 0-345-41242-7
    1. Youth—United States—Political activity.   2. Political
participation—United States.   3. Lobbying—United States.
I. Title.
HQ799.2.P6S43   1997
303.4—dc21   97-16733
                                                            CIP

Text design by Holly Johnson

Cover design by Kayley LeFaiver
Cover photo by James Wasserman

Manufactured in the United States of America

Printed on recycled paper

First Edition: September 1997

10 9 8 7 6 5 4

To Melissa
Our friendship is a good thing.

Acknowledgments

I would like to thank all the people who have guided and supported me throughout my career.

I would also like to express special thanks to my brilliant agent, Joe Regal, at Russell & Volkening; to my editor, Andrea Schulz, at Ballantine; to my friend and adviser, Riki Robbins; to my family and friends; and to the thousands of people who send me letters and stop me at airports to tell me all the good stuff they're doing to help our planet.

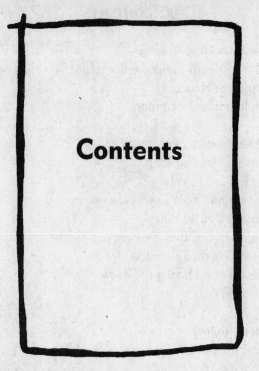

Contents

A journey of a thousand miles must begin with a single step.
　　　　　　　　　　　—Lao-tzu, *The Way of Lao-tzu*

Foreword

Long before I wanted to be an actor, I wanted to be a leader and make a difference in my community. I took on my first major project in high school when I started Students Serving Seniors, a program that matched up students from my school with local senior citizens who needed help with chores or errands or just some company.

Four years ago, I helped start another organization called Do Something. Do Something's goal is healthy communities. We believe that young people have the energy and vision to play a role in improving their communities. To that end, we have created a number of programs that inspire and support young leaders around the country.

The Do Something $500 Local Grants provide young

people with the financial assistance to take the first step toward becoming leaders. The Brick Award for Community Leadership awards $200,000 to the best community leaders in the country. Our Grand Prize Winner and nine grantees are making significant, measurable contributions to their communities, and they are all under the age of thirty!

As an organization, Do Something has experienced tremendous growth over the last four years. We have had the opportunity to work with many young leaders and have watched communities become stronger because of their work. Danny Seo is one of those dynamic young leaders. His hard work, dedication, and leadership have made his community a healthier place to live.

Generation React: Activism for Beginners takes Danny's work as a leader to the next level. He shares his knowledge with you so you can take the first step toward becoming a leader and realize your hopes and dreams for your community.

Whether "change" means working with seniors or protecting the environment, it occurs locally and *everyone* has the power to create it. Use Danny's accumulated strategies and do something. Your future and everyone around you will be better for it.

Andrew Shue

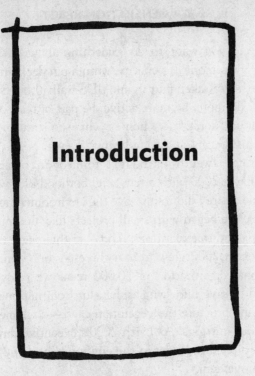

Introduction

Have you noticed? Our generation faces problems that didn't exist when our parents were our age. Millions of people are now infected with HIV/ AIDS while thousands die every day waiting for a cure. The national deficit has climbed to an astronomical level (at last count, it was around three trillion dollars). Schools have become war zones where security guards and metal detectors routinely check students for weapons. So it's not surprising that many of us feel hopeless about the future.

What can you do? Well, despite the bleak news, there is a glimmer of hope. Take yourself, for example. You picked up this book because you know what's happening to the world and you want to do something about it. Perhaps you've given money to charity, worn a pin declaring "Save the Earth!" or taken part in an AIDS walkathon. Still, you want to do more, be more active, be part of real solutions, but you just don't know how or where to start. How do I know this? Because I used to be just like you.

On my twelfth birthday I formed an organization called Earth 2000 with a few neighborhood kids who had the same desire I did to improve the environment and help animals. We began with small projects like aluminum can recycling and tree plantings. And over the course of seven years, Earth 2000 grew from a three-person operation to a national organization of 20,000 teens who have campaigned to save pilot whales, ban fur from national retail stores, and promote the vegetarian cause—to name only a few of our missions. As Earth 2000's executive director, I became a teenage leader in the environmental and animal rights movement.

Because of all the publicity Earth 2000 has received, I get thousands of letters every year from teenagers all over the world asking me the same question: "How did you do it all at such a young age?" Despite my successes, I didn't know the answer, and I always told them to find a book on activism. Then I learned something surprising: There were no books on how to be an activist. So I decided to write one.

I wrote *Generation React* to help concerned young people from any political or social background—whether you're pro-choice or pro-life, animal righteous or human righteous, liberal or conservative—change the world. You will learn my secret fund-raising tips. You will find out how to start an organization and how to infiltrate "sluggish" groups. You will learn how to change school policies. You will master the real way to get publicity. You will find out how to conduct a consumer boycott campaign so effectively that a corporation will change its destructive business practices. And you will get direct advice on how to be an effective one-person activist. In addition, I share some "must know" skills that I have developed and depend on for my successful campaigns. I've also included in each chapter my thoughts about my favorite Earth 2000 campaigns to give you insight into my life as a teen activist. In short, this is the ultimate guide to activism for beginners.

I have learned, after launching dozens of campaigns and speaking to thousands of teens, that if all of us start taking action, we can change the world. If I can change from a naive, uncaring teenager into the executive director of a powerful youth-advocacy group, then you can improve your school, neighborhood, or town.

Don't let the thought of working to solve social ills scare you. Any steps you take toward your goal, even the tiny ones, will make you a stronger person. You'll see it's not a difficult thing to do. Trust me. Now is the time to leave the apathetic comfort of Generation X and become a part of a generation of people who are reacting to the world's problems and changing the future. This book will help you in your metamorphosis from worrier to warrior.

Chapter One

Organization 101

I f you're like a lot of people, you'd like to contribute something positive to society. Perhaps you'd like to revive a neighborhood park, help homeless cats and dogs, or fight drug abuse in your community. And even though you know you should be more active in helping to solve these problems, you never get around to doing anything; it seems like too much work. But contrary to popular belief, making a difference in the world around you can be very easy if you do one simple thing: Start with small, realistic, tangible goals.

To begin: Tune into the television nightly news ("Entertainment Tonight" does not count) and watch the entire program from start to finish. Ask yourself: Which stories make me cry? Which stories make me angry? Which stories make me pay attention? Write your answers on a piece of paper and ask yourself the same questions when reading a newspaper or a newsmagazine like *Newsweek* or *U.S. News & World Report*. Be sure to take careful notes.

Do you see a pattern to your answers? For example, if the stories that caught your attention were all related to environmental issues, like an oil spill in the Atlantic Ocean and an ancient forest clear-cut in Washington state, then you have a pattern. On the other hand, if your answers are diverse—a story about gunfire in Los Angeles and an article about federal welfare cuts—then you need to narrow your focus. Choose the topic that meant the most to you and make that your project.

Once you've completed that step, ask yourself: What specific issue in this topic do I want to work on? For example, if your topic is gun control, perhaps your goal can be reducing the number of handguns brought into your city's schools. That's specific. But if your goal is to ban all guns in the United States, your scope is too broad. The more particular you can be about your goals, the better. Take your time and be thorough. Most important, be definitive.

101

Now that you've narrowed your focus to a specific goal, you're ready to be an activist. But before you take your demands to City Hall, you need to learn how most activists and organizations get the job done. Welcome to Activist University.

Ninety-nine percent of all social change is achieved

by an organized group of individuals working together toward a common goal. A small minority of these groups are large, national organizations boasting millions of members with big bank accounts. But most of the important work being done on behalf of "the cold, the tired, and the hungry" is handled by grassroots organizations and their volunteers. They make a big difference with their small, individual efforts to solve the bigger, pressing problems.

WHAT'S A GRASSROOTS ORGANIZATION?

A grassroots organization, as the name suggests, is a group of dedicated individuals working to solve social ills by attacking them at their "roots." For example, grassroots animal advocates may physically capture stray cats and dogs for a spay/neuter program. Grassroots antipoverty activists may walk the streets late at night providing free counseling and food for the homeless. Unlike the paid staff members of national organizations, these activists volunteer their time; they are not paid for their services. In my opinion, these people fit the definition of a hero: people who donate their time and energy to make the world a better place to live.

There are thousands of grassroots organizations throughout the world, ranging from two individuals working as a team to fix up a neighborhood park to huge, regional organizations boasting a board of directors and hundreds of volunteers dedicated to feeding the city's homeless. But even with clear differences in numbers and size, all of these groups share a common bond: They all saw the need to solve a pressing problem.

EARTH 2000 IS BORN

My own grassroots organization was born the night before my twelfth birthday. The night before, at midnight, trying not to disturb my sleeping parents, I snuck down the stairs to eat the last chicken salad sandwich. While eating, I turned on the television. After passing through a few station test patterns and the Home Shopping Network, I landed at the beginning of a talk show, "The Morton Downey Jr. Show."

I, like most kids in America, was never allowed to watch television late at night. Being thus denied late-night television forced me to formulate my own theories about the racy shows airing at that hour. You can imagine my disappointment when all I found was a loud-mouthed cigarette-smoking host (standing in an equally scary audience) arguing with a British woman over something having to do with rabbits and a cure for cancer. Intrigued, I took a bite of my sandwich and tried to make sense out of what was going on.

The topic was animal rights and the woman's name was Ingrid Newkirk. She supported animal rights so much that she founded People for the Ethical Treatment of Animals—also known as PETA—a national animal rights advocacy organization. I liked her immediately. The host and the majority of the audience, on the other hand, did not like her and showed it by screaming vulgar comments at her. Surprisingly, despite the continued barrage of immature and rude comments, she stayed calm and cool. I, on the other hand, was so upset over the infantile behavior of the host and audience that I declared, "I support animal rights!"— and ate a piece of chicken that fell off my day-old sandwich. Obviously, I wasn't sure what animal rights meant.

I soon learned. Ingrid looked into the audience and said that when it comes to pain, a pig and a boy feel the same level of anguish. I thought about her comment, looked at the crumbs on the floor from my sandwich, envisioned a chicken being slaughtered for my meal . . . and a few seconds later, vomited right into the downstairs toilet. My mind, body, and soul had decided that it was wrong to eat that chicken salad sandwich because an animal had been tortured and abused.

Growing up in Pennsylvania Dutch country, where vegetarianism is scarce (a local Amish diner called their one vegetarian dish "The New Age") and where slaughterhouses and factory farming are common, I never thought about exploring my dietary choices. It never occurred to me that my steak dinners, veal piccata, and chicken salad sandwiches had come from "farm" animals. I grew up eating meat; it was a staple in my diet. And I bet it never crossed my parents' minds to explain meat eating to me; it was just a part of life, like drinking water and breathing clean air. Yet I was constantly reminded by my father *why* eating meat was a luxury: When he was a child in South Korea, meat was expensive; he grew up "suffering" on a mostly vegetarian diet. We ate meat in part because of guilt.

After lifting my head out of the toilet, I knew it was my mission to help animals and their environment by stopping my own cruel and destructive ways of living. I decided to adopt a plant-based vegetarian diet. That night, I also decided to start a group, to call it Earth 2000, and to use it to tell other kids my age that animals are part of our *community*, and not a *commodity* to be exploited. The "2000" part of the name signified that I intended to save the planet by the end of the century. No problem, I thought to myself. After all, I had plenty of friends and a whopping $10 (which was a lot of money to an eleven-year-old in those days) to spend on this new project. Feeling better, I went up to my room and back to sleep.

The next day, I told all my friends not to give me gifts for my birthday. I didn't want a Swatch watch or a Teenage Mutant Ninja Turtle action figure. Instead, I wanted them to join Earth 2000 as pioneer members. Many were enthusiastic about my plans and were ready to free animals from nearby factory farms, while some were joyous simply because they got to keep my birthday presents for themselves.

On that day, an organization consisting of a handful of neighborhood kids, who collectively had $23.57 to spend, started working to save the planet by the year 2000. Sure, we couldn't drive—heck, we couldn't even cross the street—but we had the three things every great activist group needs: dedication, enthusiasm, and tenacity. And on top of that, we were young and didn't have jobs, bills, or any of the other annoying things adults always fret about. On April 21, 1989, the Earth 2000 Crusades began.

These "crusades" accomplished a lot despite their modest beginnings. From waging controversial campaigns against a development corporation to launching award-winning antifur consumer boycott campaigns, the seed I planted in 1989 has grown into a large, impressive national movement. We have proved that young people have the tenacity, intelligence, and enthusiasm to make a real, lasting difference in the world. You'll learn more about specific campaigns later in the book.

I WANT TO START A GRASSROOTS ORGANIZATION, TOO!

Whoa . . . slow down, Speed Racer! Before you jump right in and start a brand-new organization, consider exploring these *easier* alternatives:

JOIN AN EXISTING ORGANIZATION. If you see a problem you want to solve, chances are others have seen it, too. Look around your community: Is there already a group working on your issue? If there is, join and offer your time and ideas. This way, you'll be able to devote more energy to the root cause of the problem and less to constructing a new organization. It is counterproductive to have two organizations working on the same problem. There is power in numbers.

MAKE ALLIANCES WITH OTHER GROUPS. If there isn't a group working directly on your issue, consider joining an organization you think might be interested in broadening its mission. For example, if your goal is to provide meals for the homeless, you could join a local vegetarian society. You could convince them to start a program (which you enthusiastically volunteer to coordinate) to cook vegetarian meals for the less fortunate. Always be on the lookout for ways to contribute to and broaden the mission of other community organizations.

INFILTRATE INACTIVE ORGANIZATIONS. I know. It sounds like a sneaky, evil way to abuse a nonprofit organization. But community groups often lose their freshness and spunk when they've been around for a few years. When an existing organization is spending its funds on new stationery instead of on their original mission, it is time to infiltrate them. In a way, you are doing them a favor.

YOUR MISSION, IF YOU DECIDE TO ACCEPT IT . . .

Many groups, ranging from campus-based to big-name national organizations, have, at one time or another, been given new life because new, action-oriented individuals have signed on. In my opinion, infiltrations are a good thing when done for the sake of the organization's work.

For example, when an animal shelter was no longer taking a proactive role in other animal issues (e.g., fur coats, hunting), local activists ran for positions on the shelter's board of directors. As the activists slowly won executive positions, the organization refocused its mission and became an advocacy force for animal rights while continuing the shelter operations.

Dozens of campus-based groups are similarly in need of reform. Some examples:

• Infiltrate a tree-hugging, "feel-good" campus environmental group to make it more active in local ecological issues.

• Take over your student government association by running for an executive position. When in power, earmark funds for worthy community programs and not for parties and dances.

• Even athletic teams can be reformed. A water polo team could lead a campaign against water pollution; the football team could raise money for a local shelter.

The list goes on and on.

Many community-based organizations are also ripe for reform. Some ideas are:

• Convince a local women's social committee, like a gardening club, to give funds to charity instead of spending them on their regular Sunday brunch.

• Persuade a local country club or golf club to organize a charity golf tournament. Funds raised could be used to benefit local cash-poor charities.

• A local bicycling club could add trail conservation to its agenda.

The task is simple: Just present ideas to existing organizations and help them tailor your new project into their area of interest.

An important rule to remember: You should only infiltrate inactive organizations. For example, an environmental group whose main objective is to hand out "Save the Earth!" pins needs to be infiltrated. But an organization for the homeless that already provides a soup kitchen, showers and laundry, and free medical assistance does not. You do not want your role as an infiltrator to be perceived negatively. If your efforts to reform an organization are seen by others as a positive step forward, then you are not overstepping any boundaries. Look. Listen. Infiltrate.

HOW TO START A GRASSROOTS ORGANIZATION

You've searched high and low in your community for a group to join and you come up empty-handed. So you decide to start your own group.

Starting a new grassroots organization is easy. It only takes two elements: a leader to guide the organization and a few friends to help out when needed. Keeping it running, however, takes a lot of time and dedication. Remember, when you start an organization, you are pledging to stick through the good, the bad, and the ugly times your organization will face. Too many activists have an "I know when to leave a sinking ship" attitude. This is poor discipline. People who are always creating new organizations are probably doing it for the notoriety and are not likely to be around when the going gets tough. Rome wasn't built in a day and you won't change the world overnight.

FINDING INTERESTED INDIVIDUALS

Perhaps the hardest part of starting a new organization is finding people to join it. It's even harder when you live in a rural community, where the entire population equals that of a New York City apartment complex. Whatever your geographical location, you can use the following tactics to attract prospective members.

SEND OUT A NEWS RELEASE. Using the sample news release on page 11 as a guide, write a news release and mail or fax it to the local media—television, radio, and print. Be sure to include an explanation of how individuals can join your group. In larger cities like New York

For Immediate Release
Contact: Jennifer Patterson or John Morrison
@ 212/555-1111
August 20, 1997

New Youth Group Encourages Teens to Shoot Up
Not Drugs, but Basketballs in New Youth After-Hours Club

New York, NY—When 18-year-old Jennifer Patterson lost her best friend to a heroin overdose last year, she decided to do something about New York City's growing drug problem. When 17-year-old John Morrison saw "one too many" classmates doing every drug from marijuana to LSD, he knew he had to stop them. So when the two got together to come up with a plan, they decided to shoot up. No, not drugs—basketballs.

"I think a lot of young people get involved with drugs because there's nothing else to do," says Shoot Up! cofounder Jennifer Patterson. "I saw my friends start drinking alcohol, then they would experiment with pot, and then move on to hard drugs like LSD and heroin. I've lost a friend and want to prevent this happening to other teens."

The organization, founded in early August, has been highly successful. More than 200 students have signed up for the program, which meets on Friday and Saturday nights, when most kids fall prey to peer pressure to try drugs. "We meet at Parkfield High School and have activities like basketball, volleyball, watch movies. . . . It's a lot of fun. People don't see it as a goody-good thing, but as a really great place to hang out and chill," says cofounder John Morrison.

The group is looking for interested adults and businesses to help out. Donations like sports equipment, televisions, and refreshments are needed in addition to monetary donations. Also, volunteers are needed to help coordinate events. To help out, interested individuals and businesses can contact Shoot Up! c/o Parkfield High School, 101 Main Street, New York, NY 10020.

###

and Washington, D.C., your news release will have to be a real eye-catcher, since it will be only one of many. Consider using attention-getting headlines like "New Community-Service Group to Attack Root of New York's Poverty." Be creative. The media in smaller communities have fewer stories fighting for space and are more likely to run your news release as written. Also, small-town newspapers are always hungry for news; your brand-new organization may end up as a feature article instead of a blurb. Study my sample and use it as a guide for yours.

TIP: To track the effectiveness of your new-member media campaign, assign a "department code" to your mailing address. For example, when an article about Earth 2000 appeared in *React* magazine, our address read: Earth 2000, P.O. Box 24, Dept. R, Shillington, PA 19607. We could tell how many *React* readers became new members by counting the number of "Dept. R" inquiries we received.

ATTEND COMMUNITY EVENTS. Find out what special events and festivals are happening in your community and set up an information booth at as many of them as possible. (If there is a fee to set up a stand, don't attend; you can't waste valuable funds on exhibition fees.) Distribute flyers about your group that contain the following information: the group's mission, a contact phone number and/or address, and a contact name for prospective members. Also, have a sign-up sheet so people can join right away.

POST SIGNS. Make hundreds of photocopies of a sign about your newly created organization. Be sure to include a phone number and/or address. Post signs in high-traffic places like coffeehouses, supermarkets, and community and school bulletin boards.

CAMPUS MEDIA. Advertise your group on your high school's morning announcements, television program, or newspaper. Look for available media outlets and saturate them.

PUTTING YOUR GROUP INTO FIRST GEAR

After signing up a handful of people, the first order of business should be to find a place to meet. Never, ever, use your or someone else's home as a meeting site. Using permanent, centrally located meeting places helps you avoid future problems like lack of parking space. Consider the following:

COLLEGES. Contact the public relations office of a nearby college and ask to use a classroom for meetings. Most colleges offer rooms to local organizations free of charge. A college is an ideal location: Ample parking and on-site resources like rest rooms and eating facilities make it convenient and easy for everyone.

CORPORATE HEADQUARTERS. Many corporations have conference rooms available. Contact the public relations office of a nearby corporation and ask about their policy of sharing meeting rooms with community organizations. If a member is employed by that corporation, your chances of receiving a room improve greatly.

OFFICES OF OTHER NONPROFIT GROUPS. Ask like-minded organizations (e.g. church, animal shelter) if you can borrow their office space during nonoffice hours. Contact the head person to inquire about using their facilities.

IMPORTANT TIP: Never, ever, pay money to use a room. If a college, corporation, or nonprofit group demands monetary compensation, turn them down. No community service organization should have to pay for meeting space. It is simply not worth it.

I'D LIKE TO BRING THIS MEETING TO ORDER

Once you've booked a room and signed up a handful of enthusiastic members, your next important step is to build the group's basic structure.

Every organization, whether it's the ultra-conservative Christian Coalition or the ultra-radical Feminists for Animal Rights, has the same basic working structure. I call it the generic structure because I see it used a lot and it works for most new groups. At your first meeting, use the following questions (listed in a logical, step-by-step order) to establish your "structure."

What is the mission?

Because you are the founder of the organization, you should establish the mission of the group. So this is not a question you want to ask your membership; you'll risk individuals taking radical action to redirect your original goals. Instead, ask *and immediately answer* this question with the mission statement that you have prepared ahead of time. In other words, *you* are determining the organization's mission. In this way, everyone knows the group's goal up front, and anyone who wants to can leave the group at the beginning. It's a good way to weed out those individuals who really don't care about the organization's goals.

Who will be the leader?

You should be the president of the group. Because you had the energy to start the organization, you should assume control. Accept nominations for vice president (this should be a person who already understands the group's mission; a close friend is a good nominee), treasurer (someone who is honest, trustworthy, and good with money), and a secretary (a no-brainer job that involves taking notes during meetings and writing letters). Nominees should give a one-minute presentation as to why they are the best person for the job. Have a quick election and congratulate the winners.

How will your group make decisions?

I think a majority vote is the best way for an organization to make decisions. For example, if President Melissa Hicks wants to launch a clothing drive for the homeless, she should make a short presentation about the project at a regular meeting. If more than half the members support the project, it wins. If not, it loses. Most people like this approach.

How much funding do you need?

This is a tough question. Since you don't have a crystal ball or psychic powers (and if you do, then you knew I'd ask this question), you need a general estimate as to how much you'll need in the first year. I suggest that the board meet separately to discuss the issue further and then present its findings at the next regular meeting. You can also use the skills in Chapter 2 to raise some quick funds.

When and how often will the group meet?

I put this question later for a reason: You now have a feel for how much input your members give at meetings. Members who offer a lot of suggestions take up a lot of time. People who simply listen (I call them followers) use up very little time. It's a tough call to figure out how long the meetings should last, but try your best to keep the meetings short enough for busy folks and long enough for those who love to talk. Good meeting times for campus-based groups are before the first class, during lunch, and immediately after school. Having a meeting once a week or every other week is best; once a month is sporadic. Always avoid having meetings on Mondays and Fridays—people will forget.

What's your first project?

It depends. If your organization has a very specific mission—for example, starting a recycling center in your school district—you've narrowed down your choices for the first project. But if you're like most campus organizations, your goal is to tackle a worldwide problem like human rights, hunger, or the environment. If this is the case, let members submit their project ideas in writing in as much detail as possible and use the next meeting to discuss them. Use majority rule to determine which project prevails.

What's the group's official name?

Your group needs a name that is catchy, easily understandable, and liked by the group's members. People become attached to a name, so be sure to pick the perfect name in the beginning. Avoid using acronyms (e.g., Students Working Against Poverty, or SWAP); I think it's overdone by too many grassroots groups. Try to use catchy, short names. Be careful about making the name a priority issue; your work and actions should be your top priority.

TAKING BABY STEPS

You've got your members, you've got your basic structure, and you've got your regular meeting place. So, I bet you're thinking to yourself, Now what?!?

No successful group begins as a powerhouse organization; most begin with small projects, like collecting cans of food for a soup kitchen or distributing drug awareness flyers in the community. But if every new organization starts doing small projects, why do some stay small while others become big and powerful, like Greenpeace? Simple: Some groups are happy doing tiny projects and therefore remain small; others launch larger and larger projects and become big and powerful.

Making your organization an influential force in your school or community isn't hard to do. Sure, most of us will never see our group turn into the next National Organization for Women, or Greenpeace, but you can still benefit from these five tips on becoming a powerful campus group.

DICTATORSHIPS WORK. If you're having trouble finding competent people to fill positions in your group, try a dictatorship. Despite what may be politically correct, I believe a truly successful organization must start with a leader who handles 80 to 90 percent of the work in the first year. A new organization must fulfill all of its obligations—fund-raising, campaign work, and outreach activities—completely. If the work is delegated among several individuals, chances are something will not be done properly. The leader should be responsible for deciding how funds will be spent, when volunteers should meet, and what projects the organization will pursue in the first year. He or she should also lead the regular group meetings and set the agenda. After one year of so-called dictatorship, the organization can begin to delegate jobs to individuals who have proven themselves competent and responsible.

ATTEMPT REALISTIC PROJECTS. Groups that choose to pursue difficult goals (e.g., plant one million trees by the end of the year), will have a lot of disappointed members.

Your first effort should be small in scale so it can be easily accomplished. For example, instead of trying to plant a million trees, make it your goal to plant ten trees over the course of one weekend. When you and your volunteers accomplish this task, everyone will feel empowered to take on larger, more impressive projects. By going after the "big project" right away, you risk making your members feel frustrated, overwhelmed, and unhappy.

LAY OFF THE CAMPAIGNS. If the thought of doing a campaign in your group's infancy sounds stressful, don't do one. Instead, create discussion groups or special events. For example, a vegetarian society might have a monthly potluck dinner. A human rights group might discuss ethics every Thursday night at the local coffeehouse. Once the momentum grows enough (and you'll know when it does), you can start to organize specific campaigns.

BE CONSIDERATE OF VOLUNTEERS. A volunteer is a person who offers to help or work without reward or payment. Such people are the most important asset an organization can have and they should be treated with care and compassion. If a volunteer is unable to attend a fund-raising event or staff an outreach table, *do not* get angry. I'm surprised to hear story after story of volunteers who have been "fired" by an organization's president for missing an important event. Volunteers are not slaves. People volunteer to be part of a team effort to solve real problems—not to be yelled at by a prima donna president. I've said it before and I'll say it again: You can't fire a volunteer. It contradicts the whole point of being a volunteer.

CELEBRATE. Take time to celebrate a successful project or campaign. For example, after your group wins a local campaign to stop the pollution of the nearby river, order pizza and have some fun at the end of the monthly meeting. Doing so will keep the group's enthusiasm and overall energy alive for future initiatives.

GROWTH

If your organization grows so large that it needs to hire staff members, consider becoming a 501(c)3 corporation. A 501(c)3 group is a nonprofit, tax-exempt, Internal Revenue Service–recognized corporation. Being one has benefits: lower bulk-mail postage rates and individual protection from lawsuits. It will also make donations tax deductible, and will encourage large foundations to consider your group for grants. It'll cost you a few hundred dollars to file with the IRS to become a 501(c)3, but it's worth the trouble if your group plans to hire a staff. It also takes about twenty hours to prepare the application, so you may want the help of an attorney to make sure it's completed properly. If you just plan on being a local, all-volunteer organization, don't lose any sleep over it; you don't need to file. For more information, check your local library for books about the nonprofit application process.

IT'S UP TO YOU NOW

Every grassroots organization is different. I've provided the basic blueprint to help you lay the foundation for your new organization. It's up to you to build the mission, philosophy, energy, and activism. And with the skills and secret tips in the next chapters, you will.

TOOLS OF THE TRADE

The Internet is a great place to discover new ideas and resources on grassroots activism. Check out these Web sites:

• Impact Online is a national organization helping people become more involved with other organizations nationwide through technology. Write them at: 715 Colorado Avenue, Suite 4, Palo Alto, CA 94303; or check out their Web site: http://impactonline.orgs

• See what top social leaders are doing in their communities. Check out *Who Cares* magazine's award-winning Web site: http://www.whocares.org/ You can also subscribe to *Who Cares* magazine, a journal of service and action. This quarterly magazine is devoted to educating, challenging, and inspiring people to work for positive social change. Write them at: 1511 K Street, NW, Suite 412, Washington, DC 20005; or call 800-628-1692.

• Then there's the Center for Third World Organizing. This group helps communities of color organize, develop leadership, broaden their bases of information, and build alliances with other organizations. For information about them and their magazine *Third Force*, write: 1218 East 21st Street, Oakland, CA 94606.

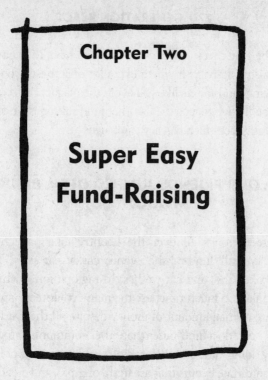

Chapter Two

Super Easy Fund-Raising

Picture yourself at a bake sale: The temperature outside is 100 degrees; the fudge brownies have melted; three volunteers forget to show up; and on top of that, nobody wants to purchase your cakes and cookies. After spending hours of your time baking, wrapping, pricing, selling, and cleaning, you've only collected a measly twenty, thirty, or—if you're really lucky—forty dollars. You think to yourself, Is this really worth it?!?

You've gotten a group of enthusiastic volunteers together to make your community a better place to live. Now you've discovered you're gonna need some cold, hard cash. Unless you've got a rich donor dying to give you a big, fat check, chances are you will have to begin some fund-raising activity. If you're like a lot of activists, you avoid organizing fund-raisers like you avoid the plague. But sooner or later you'll have to face the fact that fund-raising is a necessary part of all successful advocacy campaigns.

IF YOUR FRIENDS JUMPED OFF A BRIDGE, WOULD YOU?

Volunteer groups all over the country take part in what I call "typical" fund-raising events: candy bar sales, T-shirt sales, bake sales, and car washes. In my opinion, such "solutions" take too much time, use too many volunteers, and only generate a small amount of money despite all the hard work. Never, *ever*, do a fund-raiser that other community groups are already doing. The secret to raising significant sums of money is to coordinate events that are fresh, original, and creative. In other words, your fund-raising venture should make other groups say to themselves, "Gee, I wish I had thought of that!"

There's a common notion out there that fund-raising for community organizations has to be limited to hard, strenuous, multivolunteer events that take months of planning and coordinating. On the contrary, fund-raising doesn't have to be difficult. In my eight years of fund-raising activity, I have never stood behind a booth selling cookies, gone door to door hawking trinkets, or washed a car in the name of charity. I did, however, generate up to $2,000 a day by creating innovative fund-raising campaigns that fulfilled my three basic criteria: The project took no time to prepare, cost no money up front, and only needed one or two volunteers for completion.

I discovered these perfect fund-raisers several years

ago. In 1989, when I needed seed money for Earth 2000, I wasn't enthusiastic about the idea of selling candy bars to the public or begging my neighbors for their spare change. Instead, I wanted a quick, simple method that would raise thousands of dollars with very little effort. Like most novice activists, I thought those dream fund-raisers just weren't possible. Fortunately, I was wrong.

I discovered a fund-raising program that met my slacker requirements by mistake at a local shopping mall. Sitting by a large water fountain near the food court, I was telling a friend how I dreaded the thought of organizing a fund-raiser for Earth 2000; I wished there was an easier way to get the money. Unless I won the lottery or some mystery donor gave us thousands of dollars, I would find myself selling half-baked cookies outside the supermarket.

My friend handed me a penny and told me to make a wish. I threw the penny into the fountain, wishing for an answer to my problem and, to my amazement, I found the perfect solution: collecting coins from mall water fountains.

I knew I couldn't take my shoes and socks off and start picking up these coins. But I did know the mall staff routinely collected the coins at the end of the month when the fountains were cleaned. The only question was, Where did the coins go?

I contacted the mall management office and asked my question. To my surprise, they replied unexpectedly with, "We have dozens of buckets filled with coins in storage; do you want them?" I, almost too ecstatically, said, "Yes!"

With several friends, I wrapped thousands of pennies, nickels, dimes, and quarters (which we called gold for being so rare) into coin wrappers. After eight hours of great conversation and painless work, we raised $2,000 for Earth 2000.

Thanks to my friend's penny, I stumbled upon the perfect

way to raise funds, and it has inspired me to find other innovative ways to raise money. Here are some of my favorites.

ASK YOUR LOCAL MALL FOR FOUNTAIN COINS. Many malls in North America have indoor water fountains filled with coins earmarked for local community-service organizations. Write to the manager of your local shopping mall requesting "fountain coins" and explain how you'll spend the funds to benefit the community. Most likely, they'll approve your request, since very few groups know about the program.

After receiving the coins, ask your local bank for cloth coin sacks, *not* paper coin rolls. By bagging the coins, you can have the bank send them to the U.S. Mint to be weighed. Doing so will save you time; you don't have to hand-wrap the pennies. You'll receive a check for the full amount of the pennies in a few weeks. TIP: Hand-wrap the silver coins for quick funds. *Each bank is different. Be sure to ask them about their coinage policy.* Total funds raised: $1,000 plus.

CONSIGN OLD CLOTHING. You can make money by selling old clothing. Consignment shops sell used clothing the way an auto dealer sells used cars. To find the closest consignment shop, look under "Consignment" or "Thrift Shops" in the phone book. Call a local shop to set up an appointment and new account. Collect old clothing from your friends, family, and volunteers. Separate the pieces according to seasons—heavy jackets and sweaters for winter, shorts and T-shirts for summer—to comply with the store's requirements. Your old clothing will be sold to customers under a fifty-fifty agreement. For example, if a used jacket sells for $10 in the store, you will receive $5 and the store will keep $5. Each store is different, so shop around for the best deal. Total funds raised: $200 to $500.

COLLECT SCRAP METAL ON SPRING CLEAN-UP DAYS. One person's junk is another person's fund-raiser. Spring Clean-

Up Days allow a community's residents to dispose of large, bulky items like furniture and major appliances. Often, valuable scrap metal like brass bed headboards, copper wiring, and steel containers are thrown out. With a pickup truck, you and your friends can collect this discarded metal. Your local scrap metal dealers will pay good money for these items—they make money by selling it with other scrap metals to manufacturers for recycling. Contact a local scrap metal dealer about rates and requirements for purchase. Total funds raised: $100 plus.

ENCOURAGE YOUR LOCAL SUPERMARKET TO GIVE REBATES. In Pennsylvania, the Redner's supermarket chain gives 1 percent rebates to local community-service groups. One percent of the total grocery receipts collected by the group is refunded in the form of a monetary donation. This program is so popular that volunteers scour the store's parking lots for discarded receipts; it has become a fund-raising fixture for many community-service organizations. Contact your local supermarket to see if they offer a similar program. If not, propose they start one. Total funds raised: unlimited.

ASK A LOCAL BAKER FOR FREE PIES AND CAKES. Instead of spending hours baking your own pies and cakes (plus having to use valuable funds to buy ingredients), ask a local baker for a donation of their excess baked goods. Most companies bake hundreds or even thousands of products every day, so a donation of a hundred pies is minimal to them. Most of the time they're glad to unload excess goods by giving them back to the community; it's good PR for them. Sell the goods the same day you receive them in a high-traffic area (people, not cars!) at a reasonable price. Be sure to get permission ahead of time to set up a booth. Every penny you earn is 100 percent profit. Extra baked goods can be given to volunteers or to your local shelter. Total funds raised: $200 to $300.

ORGANIZE A TREE-ATIVITY. This fund-raising project is a Christmas tree decorating competition between several grass-roots groups. Get permission from a local shopping mall or outlet center to set up a Christmas tree display for three weeks. Each group participating is responsible for setting up a tree (live or artificial) and decorating it in the chosen theme. Donation boxes are placed in front of each tree so shoppers can vote for their favorite with monetary donations; each dollar is one "vote." All groups keep the donations they earn. The tree that gets the most "votes" (total dollar amount) wins an extra prize of $100 courtesy of the shopping mall management office. Total funds raised: $300 to $800.

SELL TREES. The National Arbor Day Foundation has a super fund-raising program that gives your group a percentage of the total sales for every tree you sell. It's simple. You collect orders from friends and family. The foundation then ships the trees to each customer via the U.S. Postal Service and guarantees that each tree will grow or be replaced free of charge. It's a one-step fund-raising program. For information, write the foundation at: 211 North 12th Street, Lincoln, NE 06508-1497. Total funds raised: $500 to $900.

CHECK THE LOCAL NEWSPAPER. Many community-service organizations offer minigrants for grassroots projects. Check your newspaper's community log and television public access announcements for word of any funding grants. Total funds raised: $200 to $500.

HOLD A RAFFLE. An in-kind good is an item donated to a charity instead of a monetary gift. Ask local businesses for in-kind goods for a raffle fund-raiser. Items like portable CD players, T-shirts, and gourmet food baskets are great prizes. Large national chain stores like Best Buy and Wal-Mart usually do not give free items to groups; it's corporate policy. Instead, ask locally based businesses. Sell tickets at $1 apiece to friends, family, and coworkers; be sure to write their name, address, and phone number on the back of each ticket. Total funds raised: $200 to $400.

CORPORATE HANDOUTS

Those of you who don't mind taking a fund-raising gamble can ask local companies and wealthy nonprofit groups for funding. It's different from the other methods because the results can be mixed. If you're great at pitching ideas to corporate decision makers, you could make a lot of money. If just the thought of talking to a company CEO scares you, you're much better off with my nontraditional fund-raising tips. But if you want to give it a try, here are the facts you'll need to get some corporate funds.

Let's Do Lunch

Many organizations hire development directors whose only job is to get major funding from corporations. They create expensive grant proposals, initiate meetings with granters, and even schmooze corporate heads with fancy dinners and gifts. This, in my opinion, is the wrong approach for the novice activist. After all, who enjoys schmoozing?

Corporate staffers who dispense grants receive a flood of slick proposals, hear the same fast talk from development directors, and receive T-shirt after T-shirt as thank-you gifts. To the corporate head, this is mundane and predictable. The *Generation React* approach to funding is totally radical and different: Let *them* discover you and your project.

GLOSSARY OF TERMS

You've got to talk the talk to get the support. Here are some terms you need to know when asking corporations for money.

Action grant: Given to fund active programs and not research projects.

Annual report: A yearly financial report prepared by the management of a corporation.

Beneficiary: The person who received the corporate gift.

Capital campaign: A fund-raising campaign extended over a period of years to raise major funds for projects.

CEO: Chief executive officer.

Donor: The business or person who makes the contribution.

Fund-raising appeal: A presentation for funds given to potential granters.

In-kind donation: A donation of physical items like computers in place of monetary donations.

Joint funding: A grant of funds that come from several sources.

Letter of intent: A document with which a corporation commits to a certain amount of funding.

Matching gift: A donation given with the understanding that the beneficiary will receive an equal amount from another funding source.

Philanthropist: A person who gives substantial amounts of money to charity.

Public charity: A tax-exempt, 501(c)3 IRS-determined organization.

Query letter: The first letter of approach to familiarize a business with a group's mission.

Unrestricted gift: A donation with no strings attached; it can be used by the beneficiary for anything.

The desire to make the world a better place is a natural human instinct. But granters feel as if they're just doing another job, not helping the planet, when they hear and see the rhetoric of professional fund-raisers. If they can "discover" your project, if you can excite them about your cause, they might want to rescue your project with a big, fat check.

I learned this just a few years ago when I placed a half-page advertisement in the program guide of the Genesis Awards, a televised awards program honoring animal-friendly movies, television shows, and journalists. I knew big-name celebrities like Pierce Brosnan, Dennis Franz, and Alicia Silverstone, in addition to major movie producers, philanthropists, and entertainment executives, attended the event. For just $400, I placed an Earth 2000 advertisement in the hands of one thousand Hollywood players, many earning multimillion-dollar salaries. And because I designed the ad myself, it lacked the slick look of professional ads, which ironically made it more appealing to the audience. The advertisment forced people to read it *because* it looked so amateurish. The ad had the right elements for a perfect "discovery" fundraiser: a wealthy, sympathetic audience and the right, downplayed look. If just one or two of these luminaries saw the ad, I believed, they would donate a few hundred dollars to support Earth 2000.

I was wrong; we raised thousands and thousands of dollars. Because I didn't assign a department code to the mailing address on the advertisement, it was impossible to know for sure how many Genesis attendees actually sent checks. But counting the returns from Hollywood and Beverly Hills alone, we raised $10,000. It was the easiest fundraiser I ever coordinated.

I've proven my theory that rich people enjoy "discovering" and funding new organizations. But since most of you probably don't have hundreds of dollars to advertise at big Hollywood events (though if you do have the cash, give it a try!), here are some hints to help you get discovered with very little money.

MAKE A PLEA IN YOUR LOCAL NEWSPAPER. Every business leader and executive I know reads the newspaper religiously. Use the media skills outlined in Chapter 3 to get an article about your group or project into the local paper. The headline of your news release should read something like "Local Project Seeks Corporate Funding" or "Highly Praised Project to End if No Funding Found." You want sympathy. With headlines like that, some corporation is bound to want to help you. Also, be sure to get an address printed at the end of the article to encourage smaller donations from readers.

GO TO THEIR PARTIES. Store grand openings, social gatherings, and your neighbor's backyard barbecue are all opportunities to be discovered by corporate executives. Introduce yourself to granters by initiating the conversation with questions about or compliments on their business. Somehow work your project into the conversation and mention it might have to end if no funding can be found. If all goes well, you'll get their business card (so you can call them Monday at the office) and a verbal agreement guaranteeing funding.

But if you're like most people, I bet you're wondering, How do I get invited to these parties, Danny? It's simple. At a regular group meeting, everyone should write down any prominent people in their neighborhood, family, or church they know on a personal basis. For example, if Mary Jones's neighbor is the director of public relations for Smalltown USA Bank, maybe Mary and you could pitch a funding idea to her.

WRITE A NONPROFESSIONAL-LOOKING LETTER TO THE COMPANY. This doesn't mean write a letter using crayons and Barbie stationery. It means writing a *personal* letter sent in a *hand-addressed* envelope. Call the company you want funding from and ask for the name of the grants/community director. Write to that person and mention in the first paragraph why you're writing; do not beat around the bush. Your letter should hook them immediately. A teenager might write, "Dear Ms. Smith: I am a thirteen-year-old kid who is tired of drugs in my school. That's why my teacher Ms. Wilson and I created a program called 'Drugs Are Wrong.' Already, some kids have stopped using drugs because of the program." The letter would then mention that the program will die if no funding arrives in the next few weeks. I ask you, what corporation would turn this request down?

FUNDING FROM NONPROFITS

Don't overlook asking like-minded national nonprofit groups for funding. Groups like The Nature Conservancy, United Way, and Greenpeace generate hundreds of millions of dollars every year. To them, a donation of $1,000 to your group is peanuts; it represents as little as .01 percent of their total available funds. Send a letter requesting funds to either the president, chief executive officer, or executive vice president of the nonprofit organization. Staff members of national organizations usually don't have the authority to dispense grants.

It is unrealistic to think you'll get funded every time you approach someone; there's a lot of competition out there for the same funds. It takes patience and determination to create the perfect marriage between a corporation and an organization. To keep you going, remember this: Corporate donations and easy fund-raisers beat a bake sale any day.

Picture yourself: It's a climate-controlled building, you're standing in a long line waiting to deposit checks totaling $5,000. You think to yourself, Boy, is this worth it!

TOOLS OF THE TRADE

• Young people (under age thirty) can apply to Do Something for $500 grants to develop a creative community-building project. For information about their Local Grants Program, write: Do Something, 423 West 55th Street, 8th Floor, New York, NY 10019; or call 212-523-1175.

WHERE TO KEEP YOUR FUNDS

All of your organization's funds should be kept in a bank checking account. Specifically, you should open an account that requires a minimum balance no larger than one hundred dollars ($100). Shop around for the best deal. Smaller banks tend to offer better deals than large, big-name institutions. If you're not careful, you could end up paying monthly fees, anywhere from $3 to $10 a month.

It should also be a joint account. That means only two people, the president and treasurer or vice president, have the power to sign and write checks.

TIP: Don't buy checks from the bank, they tend to be pricey. Instead, purchase your checks from an outside source. You have two choices:

• Affinity checks. These specialty checks support various national organizations. You can choose which organization receives a portion of your purchase. Groups benefiting include the National Organization for Women, People for the Ethical Treatment of Animals, and Greenpeace. Contact: Message!Products at 800-243-2565; or visit their Web site: http://www.greenmoney.com/message

• Economy checks. You can order checks through the mail from discount check printing companies. It only costs a few dollars to print a couple hundred checks through them. Check the Sunday newspaper coupon circular for a list of choices or contact: Current, Inc., Colorado Springs, CO 80941, for a catalog.

• The Funding Center helps nonprofit organizations worldwide in their fund-raising. For a copy of their publication *The Funding Manual: A Guide to Proposal Preparation*, contact them at: 901 King Street, Alexandria, VA 22314-3018.

• *How to Shake the New Money Tree* by Thomas G. Dunn (New York: Penguin Books, 1988), is a terrific book for the novice fund-raiser.

• Your local library probably has a section devoted to the art of fund-raising. There have been hundreds of books written on the subject. Peruse these books and pick out your favorite for ideas and inspiration.

• Check out these popular Web sites for information about grants, fund-raising opportunities, ideas, resources, and new fund-raising tactics.

> The Foundation Center: http://fdncenter.org (a terrific Web site chock-full of ideas and resources for all types of fund-raisers)
>
> Association of Grantmakers: http://www.cof.org/affinity/affinity.html

Chapter Three

Strike a Pose . . . PR!

When asked what she does for a living, Edina, the lead character in the hit British television comedy "Absolutely Fabulous," proclaims, "I PR things!" She explains that the public relations firm she owns makes a world of dull things exciting and . . . well . . . fabulous.

Creating a public relations campaign is taking the ordinary, like a rock tied with a piece of string, and making it extraordinary by calling it the Pet Rock. The public relations industry influences our buying habits, our positions on social issues, and a myriad of our other decisions. Catchy product slogans, corporate-sponsored events, and television news segments about another Wal-Mart grand opening can all be credited to public relations. If you've got a cause and you want to tell the world about it, you need to know how to turn your issue into a hot story every radio, television, and print journalist will want to cover.

MARTHA! MARTHA! MARTHA!

I never realized just how powerful the media can be until my best friend, Melissa Hicks, told me to watch a show on cable television called "Martha Stewart Living." "She's really funny," Melissa said. This thirty-minute show was hosted by an anal-retentive, perfection-loving, high-class hostess who was so self-absorbed that she named the show after herself. I learned how to make puff pastry, go fly-fishing, and create an impromptu party on the beach for unexpected guests. She's funny because she's not in touch with the average person, I thought to myself. With a little research, I soon discovered Martha headed a multimillion-dollar empire consisting of books, "signature" products ranging from house paint to cookie cutters, her own magazine, and, yes, her television show. She created this world by taking what she's good at and marketing herself as the one, and only, person who can do it. To see how effective this technique was, I decided to use my name and image to further my cause and organization.

I created media packets with headlines like "Teen Crusader Leads National Organization" and mailed out hundreds of them. I applied for national awards to bring additional credibility to my name. I faxed hundreds of news releases to cities I was visiting to generate even more coverage. During the next few weeks, journalists from various regional newspapers and magazines wrote promising articles about Earth 2000. They wrote articles *because* of me. The articles weren't just about my campaigns, but about the fact that I was a *teenager* achieving these results. To my surprise, I got hundreds of interviews. I appeared in everything from the *Wall Street Journal* to a tiny community paper in Aurora, Illinois.

Many of the articles included Earth 2000's mailing address for reader inquiries. Thinking I might receive a few responses, I was shocked to receive thousands of letters—many with monetary donations. I remember receiving 2,500 letters from just one news article!

When I started this media campaign, Earth 2000 had a few hundred members and a budget of less than $500. One year later, Earth 2000 had registered thousands of new members, hired two full-time staff members, received dozens of grants, and became the country's largest youth-oriented animal-protection group. It gave me the opportunity to write this book. I was even nominated to speak at the Democratic National Convention. I achieved my goal to become an authority on animal rights for young people nationwide.

But with every good thing comes its consequences. At Governor Mifflin High School, my alma mater, the student body and faculty had never attacked my beliefs before I started any media efforts. They believed I was just another radical hippie. As the media ran more stories about my work (thus increasing my influence), many of my fellow students believed my controversial views might have an impact in their conservative district. They gave me nicknames like "media whore" and "press slut," which I initially found amusing, then annoying, and finally upsetting. Though I lost the respect of some of my classmates and teachers, I realized it was an important sacrifice, because in addition to standing up for my beliefs, I used their resentment to fuel an even more aggressive media campaign to reach millions more individuals. At the end, my days at Governor Mifflin did teach me one important skill: how to persevere against all odds and still fight the fight.

And fight I did. I generated so much interest that I found myself placing journalists who wanted interviews on a three-month waiting list. I eventually appeared in more than five hundred media outlets. Even the *National Enquirer* ran a piece about me. Entitled "He Saved a Forest at Age 12 and Now Fights for Animals!" its subtitle called me the modern-day Noah. A week later, the same magazine said Martha Stewart was "Out to Take Over the World!" These two articles, as far-fetched as they were, caused me to realize newspapers like to write stories about people who challenge mainstream society.

The lesson of this story is simple: If you decide to become a walking billboard for a cause dear to your heart, you should expect to be both loved and hated. The result of your efforts, however, will make it worth your time and energy. Becoming an authority for your issue does more than bring your cause into the spotlight—it can also be a lot of fun. Who knows? Maybe one day you'll end up in the *National Enquirer*, next to stories about my crusade to clothe naked animals and Martha Stewart's decision to run for president of the United States.

SO HOW DO I DO IT?

If you want to get coverage in the press—a form of free advertising—you're going to have to learn the art of public relations. But relax. Starting a comprehensive media campaign involves just three simple steps: understanding basic media terminology; finding out who might be interested in your story; and making sure your efforts actually land you in the right media outlets. Invested properly, a few dollars spent on PR will reap an invaluable amount of media exposure.

TARGET ONE: YOUR LOCAL NEWSPAPER

A good cup of coffee and the morning paper are as American as apple pie. Watergate and Whitewater not only taught the American public to avoid things with aquatic names but were also brought to light by the print media. Because newspapers have the power to sway the Court of Public Opinion, they are an influential, necessary tool for any good social campaign. By winning the support of your local newspaper, your viewpoint on the issues can reach an audience of thousands.

First, here are some terms you should know:

News release: A specifically prepared statement for the press, inviting them to cover an event or story idea. (See the next section, "Writing a News Release," for more details.)

Press kit: Includes a news release, photographs, fact sheets, literature, and anything else relevant to your campaign. Some elaborate kits even include books and videotapes. Create press kits only for specific campaigns.

Media list: The full names, addresses, phone and fax numbers of journalists who are sympathetic to your cause or have already reported on your past efforts.

City desk: When you don't know where to send your news release, send it here. The city desk editor will forward your release to the reporter he or she thinks will be the most interested in your story.

WRITING A NEWS RELEASE

Writing a good news release takes a lot of time and practice, but it's worth the effort. A good release captures the attention of a reporter and can convince him or her to write a piece on your cause. Journalists, depending on the size of the newspaper, receive anywhere from a dozen to a hundred news releases every week. Your challenge is to write one that sticks out from the others. A news release can generate dozens of stories or none at all. It's up to you to figure out what gets attention and what doesn't.

Your news release should include certain catchphrases:

"For immediate release": Put this at the top of the page if it doesn't matter when the newspaper reports on your issue, or

"Embargo until": Use this if your piece is "dated." For example, if you're organizing an event on March 15 and don't want it reported until after that date, write "Embargo until March 15 @ 12:00 AM" on top of the page.

"Contact person": This is who the reporter should contact with questions—include a phone number (both day and night!) and an address.

Date of release: Always include the date that the release was written.

Title: Keep it simple but catchy. Avoid using articles like "the," "a," and "an." Study headlines in the newspaper for ideas.

Now you're ready to write the actual text of the news release.

The first paragraph should answer the four *W*'s: *Who* is organizing the event? *What* is the event for? *When* is the event going to occur? *Where* will it happen?

The second and third paragraphs should describe your efforts in more detail. Explain what you are doing and how you are doing it. Quote yourself or others involved. Include interesting facts relevant to your cause to make the story even more newsworthy.

Your last paragraph is like a biography. Discuss your educational background, interesting facts about yourself or the group, and other information that adds credibility.

End your release with "—end—" or "###."

Use the sample release on page 42 as a guide. This release was distributed to a thousand journalists and landed Earth 2000 coverage in *Newsweek* and a legion of regional newspapers.

Don't doubt yourself! If you think your news release isn't good enough (after all, *you* don't own a PR firm), don't worry. Many journalists enjoy and sometimes prefer receiving releases from individuals and community-service groups. In the era of the Information Superhighway and powerhouse PR firms, many journalists like to go back to their roots and find a hidden scoop. Most of the time, your amateur effort will appeal to this need.

A few tips:

DON'T LIE—like an elephant, a journalist never forgets.

AVOID STERILE NEWS RELEASES—to liven up the basic facts, use descriptive phrases and exciting adjectives.

DON'T BE AFRAID TO HYPE YOURSELF—though a little self-serving, it's an effective way of achieving coverage.

ALWAYS CHECK SPELLING—even the best PR firms have glarring (oops, I mean *glaring*) errors in their news releases.

While even the best news releases get ignored, it only takes one story to get a community motivated. Never, ever, give up.

[For Immediate Release]

Contact: Danny Seo @ (XXX) XXX-XXXX
Address: P.O. Box 24, Shillington, PA 19607
Date: March 1, 1995

Teen Executive Leads Teenage Crusaders

Shillington, Pennsylvania—In 1989, at the age of 12, Danny Seo planted the seed for what has become the country's largest youth-consumer organization, known as Earth 2000 National. Representing socially conscious teens passionate about animal rights and the environment, Seo and his organization have

- risked millions of dollars in a lawsuit to save a 66-acre forest from being developed
- reformed huge, billion-dollar corporations
- saved the pilot whales by launching an international boycott campaign
- promoted the vegetarian cause among Generation X'ers from coast to coast.

Seo, 17, has been so successful in organizing teens to reform Corporate America, that businesses have offered him thousands of dollars in bribes for his help in bankrupting their competition. "I've never accepted a bribe," said Seo, "but it's nice to know that our group of teens has some clout."

As the full-time, volunteer director of Earth 2000, Seo has given keynote speeches at colleges, international symposiums, and conferences normally reserved for people three times his age. In his speeches, he discusses how his generation has gotten a bad rap as unconcerned, and the success of his organization he heads proves that the young men and women of America do care about the environment and the exploitation of animals.

Seo was named "Advocate of the Year" by the American Anti-Vivisection Society and has received awards from the International Albert Schweitzer Institute for the Humanities and the Giraffe Project, which recognized Seo for ". . . sticking his neck out for the common good."

To learn more about Earth 2000, contact Danny Seo @ (XXX) XXX-XXXX.

—end—

TARGET TWO: OTHER NEWSPAPER OUTLETS

Today's newspapers provide multiple outlets for ordinary people to express their views on important social issues. In addition to news coverage, you can saturate the newspaper in sections designed to give the public a forum for discussion and opinion sharing.

LETTERS TO THE EDITOR. Write a letter to the newspaper about a recently covered topic. For example, if a local fur store placed full-page ads about an upcoming sale, write a letter about the cruelty involved in fur coats. Your letter will probably be published if it's well written. And it only costs you the price of a stamp to voice your opinion.

OP-ED PAGE. This page runs editoral pieces, usually 800 to 1,200 words in length, on current events and controversial topics. It's difficult to get an editorial printed but worth a try if your writing skills are in pretty good shape. Read previous Op-Ed pieces to get a feel for their tone. Every newspaper wants something different.

CONTRIBUTE. Smaller newspapers and newsletters will gladly accept a good writer who has interesting ideas and respects deadlines. Send an editor a list of story ideas; suggest a regular column. Don't ask for money. There isn't any.

I've Tried Everything!
Why Can't I Get Any Coverage?!?

You've worked hard on your PR campaign with no results. First, study your release. Did you put the right date and time on it? Did you remember to mail it? (You'd be surprised how many people forget to do that.) Did you give ample time for the journalist to respond? Was it an abnormally busy news week? If you've answered "no" to any of these questions, then study my two most popular media "stunts" and try to incorporate them into your campaign. They've usually worked for me.

FREE FOOD. Whenever promoting my pro-vegetarian message, I always invite journalists to vegetarian luncheons and dinners. To defend my point that vegetarian food doesn't have to taste bland, I served grilled portobello mushroom sandwiches and chocolate-covered strawberries at my last media luncheon. It was a huge success. If you plan to serve food, make it relevant to your cause. Also, don't disappoint the journalists by serving potato chips and Coke. Here are some sample food menus you can use for a variety of causes:

Breakfast foods: Bagels, fresh fruit, coffee and tea.

Luncheon foods: Gourmet sandwiches like avocado and roasted peppers with pesto on crusty French bread, with bottled water and lemon wedges.

Theme foods: Food doesn't always have to be tasty or even eaten. If you want to emphasize the low quality of food fed to children from poor families, for example, cook up what an economically disadvantaged child might eat on a daily basis; use props to show it lacks the vitamins and nutrients a growing child needs. This might be enough evidence to convince a few reporters to write against cutting welfare to poor families.

EXPLOIT YOURSELF. Find a quality unique to yourself and focus on it in your news release. A teenager might write "Teenage Crusader Leads War on Drugs." Throughout the release, the words "youth," "young people," "teens," and "adolescents" would be used repeatedly. The point is to differentiate yourself from other activists by showcasing your unique quality.

TARGET THREE: TELEVISION

Television, on a national level, is the most powerful media outlet. Oprah Winfrey, for example, reaches millions of Americans every day with her nationally syndicated talk show, "The Oprah Winfrey Show." On one show, she commented she would no longer eat red meat because she was worried about Mad Cow Disease. The next day, cattle prices plummeted on the Chicago stock exchange.

While *your* appearance on television won't cause radical changes in the stock market, you can still bring your issue to the people. But before you start your television campaign (and run to the mall for a new outfit), there are two terms you should know:

Talent booker: The person responsible for "booking" guests on television talk shows. Not all shows have talent bookers. If the show does have one, contact him or her about being a guest.

Associate producer: These people wear many hats. They're in charge of the overall direction and production of a show—and may be good people to contact about being a guest.

Getting "booked" on a local television talk show is just like getting covered in your local paper. Send the talent booker or associate producer a news release, a cover letter, and a few news clippings about yourself and/or your cause. If you've done other television shows, send a list with your media kit. To find out who the booker or producer is, call the station or purchase Bradley Communications's *Publicity Blitz,* a list of producers, writers, and editors (see "Tools of the Trade" at the end of the chapter). When composing your cover letter, make a convincing argument that your cause should be addressed on the show and that you're the person who should be addressing it. There is no room here for modesty.

If you get booked, be sure to follow these tips:

- Keep the focus on your topic and not on you. Audiences don't like guests who talk about themselves.
- Watch a few shows to get a general feel for how they flow. I recommend attending a taping or two of a nationally televised talk show to get an up close and personal look at how a talk show is produced.

"TODAY ON 'OPRAH' . . ."

The following list provides the phone numbers and addresses of popular national talk shows. The tickets are free, but some shows have longer waiting lists than others (e.g., it's much easier to get in to "The Sally Jessy Raphael Show" than it is to get in to the highly popular "Rosie O'Donnell Show").

The Geraldo Rivera Show
Geraldo Tickets
CBS Broadcast Center
524 West 57th Street
New York, NY 10019
212-265-1283

In Person with Maureen O'Boyle
NBC Ticket Office
c/o "In Person Tickets"
30 Rockefeller Plaza
New York, NY 10112
212-664-3333

The Gordon Elliott Show
Gordon Elliott Tickets
CBS Broadcast Center
524 West 57th Street
New York, NY 10019

Late Show with David Letterman
Late Show Tickets
Ed Sullivan Theater
1697 Broadway
New York, NY 10019
212-975-1003

Late Night with Conan O'Brien
NBC Ticket Office
c/o Late Night with
  Conan O'Brien Tickets
30 Rockefeller Plaza
New York, NY 10112
212-664-3056

Live! With Regis and Kathie Lee
Live Tickets
Ansonia Station
P.O. Box 777
New York, NY 10023-0777
212-456-3054

The Maury Povich Show
Maury Povich Tickets
221 West 26th Street
New York, NY 10001
212-989-3622

The Montel Williams Show
Montel Williams Tickets
433 West 53rd Street
New York, NY 10019
212-989-8101

The Ricki Lake Show
Ricki Lake Tickets
401 Fifth Avenue
New York, NY 10016
212-889-6767 ext. 758

Rolonda
Rolonda Tickets
411 East 75th Street
New York, NY 10021
212-650-2060

The Rosie O'Donnell Show
NBC Ticket Office
c/o Rosie O'Donnell
  Tickets
30 Rockefeller Plaza
New York, NY 10112
212-664-3056

The Sally Jessy Raphael Show
Sally Jessy Raphael
  Tickets
515 West 57th Street
New York, NY 10019
212-582-1722 ext. 58

• Don't wear clothes with confusing patterns; it looks strange on television. Instead, choose dark, solid-colored pieces. Never, ever, wear a white shirt.

• Wear clean clothing. The audience has preconceived notions about grungy-looking guests. Look nice. Your mom would be so proud.

• Be sure to get an address and/or phone number superimposed onto the screen so interested viewers can contact you about how they can join or help. Earth 2000 has gained thousands of members simply by appearing on a few local television programs.

• Bring a blank VHS tape with you to get a copy of the show. Most television shows are willing to provide you with a copy of the broadcast. You can show the tape to prospective members and donors. Also, watch yourself at home to see how well you presented yourself on television. Learn from your mistakes.

• If this is a live call-in show, have supporters call in with prearranged questions. I did a show in Cleveland, Ohio, without telling anyone about it. In two minutes, more than a hundred people from an opposition group flooded the lines with dead-end questions to humiliate me. Creating a positive energy about your appearance gives the impression that a majority of people support your cause.

• Never say "hi" to your friends or family. No one cares.

• Bring color photographs of your members or yourself in action. For example, bring good-quality photos of your group at a protest, doing a beach cleanup, and so on; anything to make the group seem more interesting.

• Finally, have fun! Talk to the host as if you are talking to your best friend. Remember, however, you're there to bring your cause to the people. Period.

TARGET FOUR: HITTING THE RADIO WAVES

Sitting in my bathrobe at home, I telephoned a friend to explain why I support animal rights. What might appear as a typical friend-to-friend conversation was really a nationally broadcast interview on one hundred major city radio stations. In five minutes, with almost no effort, I was able to reach millions of people with my platform. A family traveling down Route 66 heard me. A teenager in Chicago heard me. A congressman in Washington, D.C., heard me. You get the picture?

Luckily for you, a lot of people forget to send news releases to radio stations. Many people believe radio shows are passé. But I've discovered radio is a powerful media outlet. It not only generates the same response as a television talk show, but it also requires a lot less preparation (and you don't have to worry about what you wear). And radio shows allow guests to take questions direct from listeners. To get booked on a show, send your news release, cover letter, and a few news clippings to the producer of your favorite radio program.

Here are a few ways to avoid a disastrous radio interview:

• Turn off "call waiting"—it seems obvious, but it can be very embarrassing if, in the middle of a sentence, you hear that distinctive beep. (Call the operator to learn how.)

• Use a clear phone line—in other words, don't use a cordless phone; the static will drive the host and everyone listening crazy.

• Speak slowly—you'll sound more professional, and people will have a chance to process everything you say.

• Have fun—the more personable you sound, the more receptive the audience will be.

A FEW WORDS

Media exposure is necessary to raise awareness of your issue in the community. It may seem tough at first, but your dedication and perseverance will ultimately land you and your cause in the media spotlight. And if you come across as an interesting, competent person, you'll be contacted time and time again for your input on a variety of topics. You have a voice; make it heard.

TOOLS OF THE TRADE

• Read *Guerilla P.R.* by Michael Levine (New York: Harper Collins, 1993). This is the most comprehensive how-to guide on public relations available on the market today. It's my favorite PR book.

• Write to The Giraffe Project for a "giraffe" nomination packet. This nonprofit group recognizes individuals who "stick their necks out for the common good," and awards them by creating a personalized media campaign. The Giraffe Project is very competitive but well worth the effort, since many journalists look to it for stories about community heroes and leaders. A powerful resource. Write to: The Giraffe Project, P.O. Box 759, Langley, WA 98260.

• Contact Bradley Communications about their Publicity Blitz services. *Publicity Blitz* is a computerized listing of virtually every newspaper, magazine, radio and television talk show in the United States. Formatted for your computer, it comes complete with full names, addresses, and phone and fax numbers for thousands of media outlets. It makes a massive publicity campaign a cinch. Worth the investment. For your free information kit write to: Bradley Communications, 135 East Plumstead Avenue, Box 1206, Lansdowne, PA 19050-9206; or call 800-989-1400.

Chapter Four

Student Rights

In high schools all over the country, students are forming advocacy clubs, introducing resolution proposals to school boards, and writing underground newsletters to express their dissatisfaction with their schools. Teens are standing up against the old, outdated school policies of yesteryear. Through campus-based, grassroots-oriented action they're making lasting, real reforms to everything from banning classroom animal dissections to abolishing an outdated school uniform policy, from allowing campus religious groups to have Bible studies to organizing separate dances for gay and lesbian teens. Isn't it inspiring?

I did my first campaigning while still in school. When I

left Governor Mifflin Elementary School and moved up to the junior high school, I developed a fear like no other. I didn't fear a bully or the prospect of not being popular among my peers. I feared my sixth-period life science class with Mr. Hoyer.

I found it ironic that we learned about "life" science by collecting and dissecting dead animals. I was a vegetarian and a devoted animal rights advocate, but that didn't matter to Mr. Hoyer. His students were to be taught under his rules, and only his rules. No one ever challenged his system of teaching. No one.

I dissected many animals. Starfish were shredded into tiny pieces; fish became a pile of gills, fins, and scales; frogs had their entire body ripped open to expose their internal organs. I will never forget the way the smell of chemically treated animals permeated the classroom, the formaldehyde liquid that squirted onto my face, or the frog leg that projected onto my arm. It was a very painful experience.

Even though I passed the class with flying colors, I believed I failed as a person. I failed because I didn't stand up for my beliefs or for the rights of the animals. What choice did I have? I asked myself. Sure, I could've raised hell and rallied students to join my fight. I could've changed the classroom routine, fought for a student's right to refuse dissections. Any action would have been better than no action. So why did I remain silent?

Like most kids, I did not know I could stand up for my beliefs. I was young, impressionable, and naive. But a year later, I finally decided to speak up on behalf of students. If I was to cut out dissection in my school, I needed to share my story, my feelings, and my strong beliefs with the Governor Mifflin School Board. I wanted to stand up not only for animal rights but for the rights of students who wanted a humane alternative to dissection and who did not want to be reprimanded for choosing the latter option.

My speech to the school board was genuine, unrehearsed, and from the heart. But that didn't matter to them; they responded to my plea with condescending and demeaning remarks. Nobody would listen to a kid—that is, nobody except the press.

I knew the media loved to run stories about young people taking a stand on controversial issues. The media loved my story and ran front-page articles about my anti-dissection efforts. A week later, the school board was humiliated into taking action. I was allowed to make a second presentation to the board. This time, their jokes were left at the door—they knew I meant business.

Despite my efforts, the school board refused to change their policy. And even though the community was sympathetic to my efforts, my teachers were anything but understanding. Using huge chunks of time to ridicule me, a few "educators" called me a troublemaker, a radical, and even stupid. I was chided for standing up for my beliefs. Even my locker was vandalized with racial slurs. No one at my school cared, no matter how much I protested. I felt completely alone.

I wasn't alone for very long, however. I soon learned that grassroots lobbyists from the Pennsylvania Legislative Animal Network (PLAN) were working on a statewide bill to give students the option to refuse animal dissections. Perhaps I could share my personal experiences with state legislators to generate support for the bill, bringing some good out of the experience.

I granted an interview to a conservative journalist who right off the bat said, "I'm probably not going to side with you." And he didn't. I was attacked in his column for eating egg and dairy products, even though I abstained from meat. In his eyes, I was not a purist and therefore I didn't have the right to question authority. But I was smart: I turned this lemon into lemonade.

I got sympathetic elected officials to read this unsympathetic article. I wanted them to see past the complicated language of the dissection bill to discover that real kids, not statistics, would be affected by its passage. Specifically, I wanted them to see how some kids were labeled troublemakers when all they wanted was a humane alternative to animal dissections. With the hard work of PLAN, grassroots activists, and my news clippings, the bill became a statewide law a few months later, giving students in Pennsylvania the right to refuse animal dissections.

On October 16, 1996, I addressed the National Association of Biology Teachers at an Alternatives to Dissection Symposium about the pressures young people face in the classroom. I shared my story with an audience of life science teachers to show them that young people do have credible ideas and beliefs and they cannot be ignored.

GETTING STARTED: CHANGING SCHOOL POLICY

Changing school policy is easy when you carefully plan and organize your strategy. All you need to understand are two basic things: your rights as a student and citizen, and the process of lobbying for school reform. First, your rights.

Thank goodness for our Founding Fathers. Under the First Amendment of the U.S. Constitution, your right to free speech and expression are protected. According to the American Civil Liberties Union (ACLU), a national constitutional-rights advocacy group, "students may be prevented from expressing their views only when they (the students) 'materially and substantially' disrupt the work and discipline of the school." But the phrase "substantially disrupt" is vague. What may appear peaceful to a student may be interpreted as disruptive by a school official. To avoid such conflict, students should make every attempt to be as peaceful and nonconfrontational as possible while remaining assertive in defending their rights. If you need help standing up for your rights, contact the American Civil Liberties Union (check your local phone directory, call the national office [212-944-9800], or write to them at: 132 West 43rd Street, New York, NY 10036).

Here are some of your specific rights as a student according to the ACLU:

• You have the right to wear lapel buttons or pins, even if the messages on them offend someone else.

• You have the right to form a campus-based organization. If your group does not disrupt school activities, you have the right to form a group no matter how controversial the topic may be. Be sure to fill out all the proper forms to start a group. Failing to do so will give opposing administrators and teachers an opportunity to disband the group on a technicality. There is, however, one exception: Students are prohibited from using school property for organizing religious activities because of the U.S. Constitution's infamous separation of church and state.

• You have the right to distribute underground newspapers and materials. As long as the process of distributing the materials is handled without disrupting school activities, the school does not have the right to stop the flow of materials.

• You have the right to use school classrooms for clubs.

Your right to hold meetings during nonclassroom times is protected by the Equal Access Act.

• You have the right to criticize teachers and policy. Distribution of materials condemning or supporting teachers and/or school policy is protected by the Constitution.

• You do not, however, have the right to do any of these activities if you use profane or vulgar language. If you can't say it on television, you can't say it in school.

For a complete overview of your rights as a student, read *The Rights of Students* by the American Civil Liberties Union (Carbondale: Southern Illinois University Press, 1988).

LOBBYING YOUR SCHOOL

Now that you know your rights, you can lobby for school reform without fear of repercussions. While the process of changing school policy is very much like trying to pass a bill through Congress, there is one major difference: It is much easier to pass a school resolution than to pass a state or federal bill into law. There is less bureaucracy and red tape at the school district level than at any other level of government. And that's good news for students.

Before starting any school policy campaign, answer the following basic questions so that you'll understand your goals, your supporters, and your opponents. Be totally honest with yourself when answering these questions.

What is the overall goal of your campaign? What do you hope to accomplish?

Knowing your goals ahead of time will make your campaign more definitive. For example, instead of saying, "I want the school to save the environment," a realistic goal might be "I want the school to start an office-paper recycling program."

Have you met with teachers and administrators who have the power to change the questionable school policy?

It is much easier to work from the bottom up on school campaigns. Sometimes changes can be made at a non-administrative level. For example, a student's effort to implement an HIV/AIDS awareness campaign could be done through the school nurse and not through the bureaucratic administrative process.

Who are your supporters? The student body? Teachers? A special-interest group?

Knowing your supporters ahead of time will help you recruit people farther down the road. Instead of scrambling for help at the last minute, keep an army of people on hand for immediate use.

Who are your opponents? The student body? Teachers? A special-interest group?

Keep track of any opposing forces. Some people may try to infiltrate your group in an effort to strengthen their case against your efforts. You should develop a plan to respond to the concerns and actions of any opposing groups or people.

What are your personal strengths? Are you a good speaker? Writer?

Use your talents to further your efforts. If you excel at media relations, work on getting coverage in all media outlets. If you are an exceptional writer, write an article for the school newspaper and the "Letters to the Editor" section of your local newspaper.

What is your time frame? For example, if you're graduating in a few weeks, do you have ample time to commit to the effort after you've graduated?

Whatever your goals, a time frame is critical in any campaign. Knowing how much time you have to successfully launch and execute your plans will be key in developing a strategy.

Now it's time to develop a plan of action.

First, if you haven't already, meet with individuals outside of the school board who might have the power to change policy internally. Meet with teachers, the high school principal, cafeteria staff, groundskeepers . . . whoever may be in a position to help. For example, if you want vegetarian options on the cafeteria menu every day, arrange a meeting with the cafeteria supervisor. If you want a composting program, meet with the head groundskeeper.

If these people agree to your plan, way to go! If not, on to step two.

Write a letter to the chief decision makers who will be considering your request. Send a letter to the superintendent, the assistant superintendent, and the principal. Also send a letter to any teachers or staff members who might be in positions of influence. Keep a photocopy of each letter, so you can prove that you sent them.

If still no progress, move to the next steps.

DESIGN A PETITION. Across the top should be written: "We, the Undersigned," followed by your demands. For example, "We, the Undersigned, oppose the XYZ

School's dress code policy and actively support any efforts to reverse the policy." Make lines on the paper for students to place their names, addresses, and signatures. Use a computer graphics program, if possible, to make the petition look professional. Check out the sample petition on page 61, which I used in a recent antifur campaign.

MAKE ONE HUNDRED PHOTOCOPIES OF THE PETITION. Most cities now have photocopying centers that charge as little as five cents a sheet. Do not use colored paper.

RECRUIT. Find interested students to collect signatures from other classmates. Give them a one-week deadline to return signed petitions to you. Remember, as long as classes are not being disrupted, no teacher can stop you from collecting signatures.

MAKE PHOTOCOPIES OF THE SIGNED PETITIONS. Present the original petitions to the superintendent of the school with a cover letter describing (again!) what you want. Keep the photocopies for future use.

If no action is taken by the school, move to the next level. Call the main office of the school district and ask to be signed up as a speaker at the next school board meeting. If the meeting is less than a week away, sign up for the meeting after that. You need the extra time for lobbying and preparation.

WRITE A RESOLUTION. Follow the sample resolution format on page 62 and insert your demands where appropriate. I used this one in my antidissection efforts. Make fifty photocopies of the resolution. Here are the definitions of awkward words used in the sample resolution:

Whereas: In view of the fact that. . . .

Resolved: Formally decided.

We, the Undersigned,

pledge our support to Earth 2000's national campaign to ban the use of fur from the Lerner New York retail stores. We understand animals are trapped, drowned, beaten, electrocuted, gassed, and strangled to death for their coats. Therefore, we will join in with our friends and family and support a boycott of Lerner New York until the fur scam ceases.

NAME (print)　　　　ADDRESS　　　　SIGNATURE

_____

_____

_____

_____

_____

_____

_____

_____

MAIL PETITIONS TO:
Lerner New York, c/o Mr. Barry Aved (president),
460 West 33rd Street, New York, NY 10001

RESOLUTION NO. _____

PROHIBITING THE DISSECTION OF ANIMALS IN GOVERNOR MIFFLIN PUBLIC SCHOOLS

WHEREAS, the Governor Mifflin Board of Education fully endorses scientific education and presentations in the classrooms; and

WHEREAS, the Board is sensitive to student and parent objections to animal dissection in the classroom; and

WHEREAS, the Board fully recognizes the rights of students to an education that does not violate their religious and ethical beliefs and value systems; and

WHEREAS, the Medical Research Modernization Committee, the Physicians' Committee for Responsible Medicine, and the Humane Society of the United States have provided curricula that teach children about the biology and physiology of animals without requiring the death of animals; and

WHEREAS, modern tools of research such as computer-assisted mannequins, computer programs, mathematical and physical models, and videotapes have been devised that eliminate the need to use animals; and

WHEREAS, requiring students to dissect animals tends to desensitize or revolt children rather than educate them and also has the unwanted effect of discouraging sensitive students from pursuing careers in science; now, therefore, be it

RESOLVED, that the dissection of animals shall be prohibited at all course levels in Governor Mifflin Public Schools.

MEET THE SCHOOL BOARD. Get the name of every school board member and his or her mailing address. You can get this information from the main office of the school district. Send the members a copy of your resolution, a cover letter inviting them to meet with you before your presentation, and any other supporting materials. If a member wants to meet with you, set a time and place for a ten-minute meeting. Bring a group of supportive students and parents (after all, your parents *do* pay taxes and vote) and present your case in an honest, to-the-point manner.

GATHER SUPPORT. Distribute a flyer among supportive students, inviting them to attend the school board presentation. The more young people who support your cause, the better your chances will be for getting your resolution passed.

SEND OUT A NEWS RELEASE. Using the skills in Chapter 3, send out a news release to local newspapers, television news broadcasts, and radio talk shows. Be sure to include the time, date, and location of your presentation. Include a copy of the resolution with your news release.

PRESENTATION NIGHT

Don't read word for word from a written speech; it's boring. Instead, put the points you want to make in outline form and elaborate on the spot. Speak from the heart and be genuine. Have other students speak in support of your resolution. Be understanding of the school board's concerns but remain strong and assertive. Answer their questions in a nonthreatening, nondefensive, intelligent manner. Don't ever be vulgar in your language even if a board member acts in a condescending way toward you. If you act inappropriately, you risk losing the support you might have had.

If you sense that the board will not support your resolution immediately, encourage them to take the time to consider your proposal and ask them to decide its status at the next meeting. This will give you the opportunity to do more media interviews and drum up additional support.

If your resolution doesn't pass, don't worry. This is the time to compromise with the school board, to find some common ground where you can achieve some of your goals while they keep some of their outdated policy. Most adults will applaud your enthusiasm and will want to reward it by giving you something. And that something is better than nothing.

MAKING SOMETHING INTO EVERYTHING

If you were lucky enough to get some of your demands met, great job! But if you are like most people, you still want to see all your goals fulfilled. After all, nothing is ever solved by getting the job half done. Here's how to take your something and make it into everything.

SEND A THANK-YOU LETTER TO EVERYONE. Be sure to thank each school board member, the principal, superintendent, assistant superintendent, reporters who covered your story, and students who rallied behind you from the start.

TAKE WHATEVER YOU WERE ABLE TO ACHIEVE AND ACTIVELY PROMOTE IT. For example, if the school board agreed to give students the option to refuse animal dissections *only* if they request it at the beginning of the year, sign up as many students as possible at the beginning of the year. This way, the school board will see an overwhelming demand for the program and will likely pass your complete resolution giving students a year-round option to refuse dissections.

POSTERS. Design an eye-catching, colorful poster encouraging students to write letters of support to the school board. It should be no larger than 11 × 17 inches. Make plenty of photocopies and use colorful paper. Post these around the school.

CREATE A FLYER. Make hundreds of copies of a flyer summarizing your efforts. Distribute them to students between classes and during free periods.

PHYSICALLY IMPLEMENT THE FULL IDEA. For example, if you wanted the school to start a recycling program and they refused to do so, create a pilot program to show how effective and easily executed it can be. If a teenager can do it, why can't a staffed school district?

FIND OTHER SUPPORTERS. Contact like-minded national organizations, societies, and prominent activists to support your effort. Have them send letters to the school superintendent, endorsing your resolution. And, if possible, have them provide positive comments to the school board as well.

ADVERTISE IN YOUR SCHOOL. Look for ways to advertise your campaign in school publications. Does the school's fall play program have ad space available? How about the school newspaper? Football program? Orchestra performance handout? Be creative, imaginative, and spread the word.

CREATE MORE MEDIA ATTENTION. Send a follow-up news release to the local media with headlines reinforcing your idea. A sample headline might read "XYZ Reform Plan a Total Success." In the release, thank the members of the school board for their willingness to compromise, but mention your disappointment in their lack of enthusiasm to pass the entire resolution. Be kind, but tough.

At least four months after the compromise was reached, meet with the school board again. Give additional hard facts and figures to reinforce the need for the resolution. Provide letters of endorsement from national groups, students, and well-known activists. If possible, also show pictures and graphics. The more support you show, the more pressure they'll feel to pass the entire resolution. But remember, no matter how rude they may act toward you, always be professional and calm. Again, if you sense their hesitation to support your idea, ask them to hold their final decision until the next meeting. During that time, continue to send supporting materials to the board members. Keep up the pressure until your original resolution becomes a permanent school rule.

TIP: Contact the Student Environmental Action Coalition (SEAC) for a copy of their *High School Organizing Guide*. It provides tips and ideas for launching successful campus-based campaigns. Write: SEAC, P.O. Box 248, Tucson, AZ 85702; or call 520-903-0128.

NOT A STUDENT? NOT A PROBLEM!

You don't have to be a high school student to introduce a school board resolution. Use the same skills and formats to get your resolution passed through the school. You will not be allowed to circulate a petition among students during school hours, but petitions can be passed throughout the community to taxpayers in the school district. Age is irrelevant when it comes to changing school rules.

A FINAL WORD

Changing school policy is a good way to learn civics. Whether you are in the community or in the school, you have the right to speak up whenever a policy infringes on people's rights or is ethically objectionable. You are not entering a new country complete with new rules and regulations when you enter high school. Don't be intimidated by school officials; it's your world, too.

TOOLS OF THE TRADE

• Contact the American Civil Liberties Union (ACLU) for additional information about student rights. Write: ACLU, 132 West 43rd Street, New York, NY 10036.

• For a free guide to your First Amendment rights, contact the Freedom Forum by calling toll-free 800-815-5335 or write: 1101 Wilson Boulevard, Arlington, VA 22209.

• Write the Campus Outreach Opportunity League (COOL) for information about their annual COOL National Conference on Student Community Service. Acquire critical technical skills, discover new models for organizing groups, and learn how to find new resources in your campaign for change. Write: COOL, 800 21st Street, NW, Suite 427, Washington, DC 20052; or e-mail at coolconf@gwis2.circ.gwu.edu

• Subscribe to *Student Leader*, a full-color leadership newsmagazine helping students be ethical and responsible leaders. Each issue addresses how to combat apathy, deal with diversity issues, and make ethical leadership decisions, as well as offering fund-raising tips that work. Published twice a year. Write: Oxendine Publishing, P.O. Box 14081, Gainesville, FL 32604-2081; or call 904-373-6907.

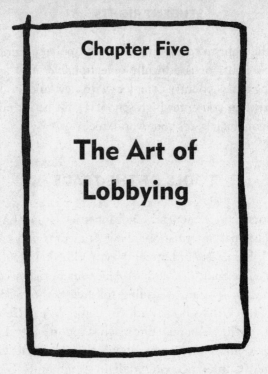

Chapter Five

The Art of Lobbying

Pop quiz. Which of the following is a lobbyist: The distinguished man in the three-piece suit working for the tobacco industry? The female college graduate working for the Children's Defense Fund? Or the radical hippie chaining himself to the flagpole outside of the White House, protesting nuclear weapons?

The answer is (drumroll, please): all of the above. If you're like most people, you probably have a preconceived notion that a lobbyist is someone who works for big businesses to make their wallets fatter and their influence greater. But not all lobbyists represent corporate greed; many work for nonprofit groups and others voluntarily lobby to support personal, closely held convictions. And yes, even the radical hippie chained to the flagpole is a lobbyist. He's just bringing attention to an issue in an unconventional, attention-grabbing way. Effective? Well, that's for the president of the United States to decide.

When a friend of mine approached me about lobbying several years ago, I hesitated. Carla thought lobbying was fun. I, on the other hand, thought meeting with politicians and reviewing "urgent" environmental legislation seemed boring and a waste of my time. I preferred working directly on environmental problems by planting hundreds of trees or launching a boycott. So each time Carla asked me to accompany her on one of her regular lobbying trips I turned her down.

I didn't think about lobbying again until a cool fall day in Green Hills, Pennsylvania, when I was standing in a field of pumpkins looking for the perfect jack-o'-lantern. As my friends ran around the three-acre field looking for the best pumpkin, I picked a shiny apple from the orchard next to the pumpkin patch. I ate it—not thinking about any possible pesticides, herbicides, or insecticides that might've been sprayed on it. After all, how much harm could one apple do?

By that night my skin had broken out into an itchy, bright red rash covering my face, neck, and back. Looking like an incredibly bad case of acne, it blistered and oozed pus every time I scratched it. I wasn't physically sick, fortunately, but I looked so hideous that my mother refused to allow me to attend school for several days.

I do not remember how long the rash lasted, but I do remember how horribly itchy and painful the experience was. To this day, I still have scars from the patches of skin I scratched open. I also have vivid memories of pouring what seemed like endless bottles of pink lotion onto my body; I looked like walking Pepto Bismol.

Several months later, after my apple phobia had passed, I was approached by my friend Carla about lobbying for a Pennsylvania bill that would require schools to limit the use of pesticides and herbicides on school grounds. It was written to protect chemically sensitive students from being harmed by chemicals like grass fertilizer and ant repellent. This time, instead of making an excuse to back out, I wanted to help. I now knew from personal experience the dangers of pesticides and what they can do to a person.

When I told Carla my apple-eating and rash story, she was intrigued. In fact, she was so interested that she booked me to speak at a news conference in Harrisburg, Pennsylvania, about my experience with food and chemical fertilizers and pesticides.

It was my very first lobbying experience. And with very little knowledge of how government worked (I didn't even know who my legislators were), I was scared. I wasn't a scientist or an expert in chemical fertilizers; I was just a regular teenager who got sick from a treated apple. To my surprise, after nervously sharing my five-minute story at the news conference, reporters and legislators were interested in what I had to say. That night, on the evening news across Pennsylvania, thousands of families saw and heard my speech urging support for this legislation. It was the easiest thing I ever did, but it achieved the greatest result: convincing several doubtful legislators to support the bill. Since that day, I've been in constant contact with my legislators about issues that concern me.

LOBBYING 101

Lobbying is a long-standing practice in state and federal legislatures. Lobbyists, representatives of both private and public groups, attempt to influence government policy in favor of the tenets of their organization. For example, a lobbyist hired by the retail industry might lobby to stop Congress from raising the minimum wage. On the other hand, a lobbyist representing a union of retail workers would try to convince Congress to raise the minimum wage. And because they can provide substantial donations to an official's reelection campaign and/or represent a significant number of registered voters in a legislator's district, lobbyists work hard to keep legislators informed of their organization's position on all pending legislation within their organization's field of interest. And even though it hurts me to admit this, a few lobbyists live by this simple motto: If you scratch my (the lobbyist's) back, I'll scratch yours (the legislator's).

WHO THEY ARE

There are three main types of lobbyists.

CORPORATE LOBBYISTS. These people are hired by corporations to fight or support laws that affect their employers' livelihood, like oil company lobbyists working for weaker environmental regulations. They are usually full-time employees who routinely meet with legislators and sometimes give substantial monetary "gifts" to the legislator's reelection fund as a show of support. In return for their gift, they hope, the congressperson will vote for laws that help their corporation.

SPECIAL INTEREST LOBBYISTS. These are employed by nonprofit organizations. For example, the National Rifle Association (NRA) lobbyists try to protect the rights of gun owners and hunters. The lobbyists hired by Handgun Control, on the other hand, work for stronger gun control, while the Fund for Animals, an animal rights organization, works to protect animals by fighting the interests of hunters. There are thousands of registered, nonprofit lobbyists working to influence laws affecting everything from the rights of children to the rights of whales. Like corporate lobbyists, special-interest groups who use lobbyists often donate money to legislators' reelection coffers through a special arm of the group called a political action committee, or PAC. Since they cannot use regular funds to support legislators due to nonprofit tax laws, these groups form a PAC funded by private contributions for the sole purpose of giving monetary gifts to legislators. They also offer cooperative congresspeople something even more appealing—the votes of the members of their organizations. Groups like the Sierra Club, with 400,000 members, and the Humane Society of the United States, with 1.1 million members, often have clout among congresspeople for this reason alone.

VOLUNTEER LOBBYISTS. These people are not paid for their services and are usually active for only one reason: They feel passionate about their cause. In their spare time, these ordinary citizens use grassroots tactics, a form of lobbying that does not involve big sums of money but instead personal actions like letter writing and press conferences, to influence legislation at the state and federal level just like paid lobbyists do. For example, a mother who lost her son to a drunk driver may lobby for stiffer drunk-driving laws. This is the type of lobbying you will learn how to do.

BREAKING DOWN THE PRECONCEIVED NOTIONS

Lobbying is stereotyped as a difficult thing to do. It's not. Lobbying is just a technical term for the simple act of expressing your views to a congressperson. In my opinion, it is one of the easiest ways an activist can make a difference, so it's worth your time to give it a try.

When I first started lobbying my state legislature, several years ago, I was petrified. I was a clueless teenager without an iota of knowledge about lobbying. I was scared to meet with my legislators and worried that my comments might hurt my cause instead of help it. But I was worried over nothing. My opinions on pending legislation had a profound effect on the voting records of my legislators. The entire lobbying experience was like a meeting with a friend. I also discovered legislators really do care about the feelings of their constituents. Even though I personally couldn't vote, I was still a very influential lobbyist, because as president of Earth 2000, I was in contact with thousands of teens throughout Pennsylvania who had parents and older siblings who did vote. My lobbyist friend Laura summed it up best when she said, "No politician wants to be known as the legislator who made a group of kids cry."

As I got older and reached the age when I could vote, more and more political forces asked me for help. The largest political camp to recruit my assistance was the Clinton/Gore '96 campaign. As a consultant and member of the Clinton/Gore Youth Steering Committee, it was my responsibility to encourage young people nationwide to support the Democratic ticket. I appeared on one national television show, gave the committee permission to use my name in news releases endorsing the Democratic Party, and offered continual advice on what today's youth cared about. I am confident the skills I learned from my first lobbying experience led me to my critical role in the Clinton/Gore '96 campaign.

TIP: Every time I felt nervous before a meeting, I said

to myself, These are public servants whose job is to serve me. I employ them. This is a true statement. Legislators are elected by the votes of the people, and their salary is paid by public tax money. They are "hired" to represent the views of their constituents. They work for us.

THE LOBBYIST DICTIONARY

As a lobbyist, there are some basic terms that you should know. They are words commonly used by elected officials, their staffs, and lobbyists. Don't use them just to impress a friend at a party; make them part of your lobbying vocabulary.

Act: A bill that has been passed by both houses and becomes law.

Bill: A proposed law introduced in either the House or Senate.

Committee: Workshops comprised of legislators who study new bills, dissect them to find problems, and hear concerns from lobbyists, constituents, and other legislators.

Constituent: A public citizen in a legislator's district.

District: A territory of the state that has one state senator and one state representative to represent its interest in the state legislature. Federal districts are larger and have one federal representative. Every state has two federal senators.

Filibuster: To deliberately take advantage of the "freedom of debate," a law allowing a legislator unlimited time to debate a bill before a vote, in order to delay the vote on a bill.

Impeachment: A proceeding brought against an elected

official for the purpose of removing that official for misbehavior in office.

Nonpartisan: Not influenced by political party bias.

PACs: Political action committees; special-interest groups (or the separate political arm of a nonprofit organization) who lobby and give campaign contributions to political candidates.

Resolution: A form of written proposal used to make declarations, state policies, or announce decisions when a bill or some other form of legislative action is not needed. For example, a legislator proclaiming Pennsylvania supports rain forest preservation needs only a resolution to get the proclamation approved. The difference between a bill and a resolution is clear: A resolution does not become a law; it is, however, a way for the legislature to make a statement about its views on an issue.

Table: To postpone action or debate on a bill. If a legislator has a special interest in a certain bill (e.g., a bill that would force cattle ranchers to pay higher taxes and the district has more cows than people), the legislator would try to table discussion—and therefore stall action—until he or she could find a way to gain support.

Veto: The power of the president of the United States and each state's governor to reject a bill that has already passed both legislative houses.

TIP: Take a field trip to your state capital and tour the capitol building. (Call first for times, dates, restrictions, etc.) The tour will familiarize you with the layout of the building, the historical aspects of government, and the workings of government in your state. It won't answer every question you have about government, but it's a good way to get your feet wet.

DOING YOUR HOMEWORK

Before you become a grassroots lobbyist, you have to understand the basic process of how an idea becomes a law. There are many steps in the lawmaking process, which is designed to question the need for and the effectiveness of a proposed law. The deliberate slowness allows for open discussion and provides many opportunities for the general public to influence the shape of the final legislation. Here's how an idea becomes a law at the state level.

First, a member of the general assembly, the official name for the entire body of all state legislatures, writes a bill. The legislator now looks for other legislators to co-sponsor the bill so it will have a better chance of passing. It's like the bandwagon theory: The more co-sponsors a bill has, the better chance it has of gaining support because of internal peer pressure.

The bill is then introduced to the general assembly and sent to the appropriate committee for review and public distribution, which is the process of informing the general public about the pending legislation.

Once committee members have reviewed the bill— and after hearing the concerns of constituents, lobbyists, and other legislators—they will either leave the bill alone or amend (change) it. Changes will be made if the majority of the committee feels clarifying measures or words need to be added. These changes are made to solve any problems the original bill did not address. The bill can also be tabled, which is the process of ignoring legislation—in other words, killing the bill.

Once out of committee, the bill is reintroduced, with its changes, in the Senate or House, depending on where the bill orginated, for vote. For our purposes, let's say it originated in the Senate. The bill is then voted on by the Senate.

After the bill passes the Senate by majority vote, it is transmitted to the House, where it is assigned to a House committee. The House committee may make changes or table the bill. Any changes made by the House must be approved by the Senate. If the Senate approves them, then the bill is voted on by the House. If the changes are not approved by the Senate, then further changes can be made by both sides until the bill is acceptable to both the House and the Senate.

If the bill passes both houses, it is signed by the president of the Senate and the Speaker of the House. It is then transmitted to the governor for his consideration.

If the governor signs the bill, it becomes law. If the governor rejects the bill, it is returned to the house of origin with the governor's reason for veto. The veto can be overturned with a two-thirds majority vote of each house.

If the governor takes no action on the bill within ten calendar days after he/she has received it, and the general assembly is still in session, it automatically becomes law.

The official certified copy of each bill approved by the governor is placed in the custody of the secretary of the state, given an act number, and filed with the State Department.

Phew!

LIKE . . . WHAT?

If, after reading the (dare I say) simplified version of how a bill becomes a law, you're still a bit confused about the legislative process, don't worry. I've been lobbying for several years now, and I'm still learning how government works. All you really need is a *basic* understanding of the bill process, to know who your state and federal legislators are, and what bill in your field of interest is being circulated among congresspeople in Washington and in your state capital.

In the Commonwealth of Pennsylvania, about five thousand bills are introduced every two years. Amazing. And every day, bills are made into law without the public taking much notice. There are hundreds of regulations passed every year, many of which go completely unnoticed by ordinary people like you and me. We read about a new law in the Sunday newspaper only after it's too late to take any action. What's a frustrated, ordinary citizen to do?

There are several steps you can take to stay informed about bills pending at the state and federal levels. If you are already working on a special cause (e.g., abortion rights or gun control), you can join a like-minded special interest group that will keep you informed of bills on that subject. Usually, these organizations will send you a quarterly or monthly newsletter listing the pending bills, including the bill's identification number and even the names of the legislators who either support or oppose the bill. There's even a long-distance phone carrier who can keep you updated on new and pending federal legislation. Here is a sample of five national political action organizations:

THE FUND FOR ANIMALS. This national antihunting organization has full-time lobbyists working at both the state and national levels on issues concerning animals, specifically hunting and trapping. They publish an annual report that ranks federal officials on their voting record, and produce action alerts and newsletters for their members, notifying them of current legislative efforts. Contact: The Fund for Animals, 850 Sligo Avenue, #300, Silver Spring, MD 20910.

CHILDREN'S DEFENSE FUND. This national nonprofit group exists to provide a strong and effective voice for all children of America, "who cannot vote, lobby, or speak for themselves." The Office of Government Affairs tracks key legislative proposals addressing children's issues: health care, child care, and Head Start, to name a few. Members receive action alerts on issues concerning child advocacy. Contact: Children's Defense Fund, 25 E Street, NW, Washington, DC 20001.

LEAGUE OF CONSERVATION VOTERS. This is a nonpartisan, national political campaign committee that actively promotes the election of public officials who work for a healthy environment. They evaluate environmental voting records of congressional members and presidential candidates. The highest score, 100 percent, indicates an elected official who is a staunch protector of the environment. Contact: League of Conservation Voters, 1150 Connecticut Avenue, Suite 201, Washington, DC 20036.

PUBLIC CITIZEN. This is a national organization working to fight the "special interests" of powerful corporations in government. Founded in 1971 by activist and 1996 Green Party presidential candidate Ralph Nader, Public Citizen comprises ordinary citizens banding together to defend democracy and to protect themselves from the tyranny of the rich and powerful. Contact: Public Citizen, 2000 P Street, NW, Washington, DC 20036.

WORKING ASSETS. This is the nation's leading *socially responsible* long-distance phone service company that not only gives a percentage of your monthly phone bill to nonprofit groups like Greenpeace and Planned Parenthood but also keeps you informed of upcoming bills on political and social issues where your voice can influence the outcome. Each telephone bill (printed on recycled paper) highlights a specific bill in Congress that may interest you. Working Assets even foots the bill for your phone call to your legislator in Washington. Not bad for a phone company. Contact: Working Assets, 800-788-8588; or visit their Web site: http://www.wald.com

Once you've discovered a bill that concerns you, you can receive copies of it by contacting your elected official's district office (be sure to contact state officials for state bills, federal officials for federal bills), or call the House Document Office for copies. Be sure to have the bill number available (usually stated in a group's action alert). If you don't know the bill number, call your legislator's office for assistance.

GETTING STARTED

First, make a list of your state and federal legislators. If you don't know who they are, contact your local League of Women Voters (LWV). The LWV is a national organization working to promote active participation of citizens in government. They can provide you with a list of your elected officials, including their addresses, phone and fax numbers, and other useful information. The LWV can help you with voter registration as well as general questions about the political process. You can also contact the Chief Clerk's Office in your state capital for a complete list of current state officials.

IT'S MEETING TIME

Once you have a list of your elected officials, you need to make appointments with them. Setting up a meeting is easy. Call the legislator's local district office (look in the blue pages of your phone book). Legislators commute regularly between their main and district offices, so setting up a meeting date shouldn't be difficult.

All you'll need is a fifteen-minute appointment, and be flexible on times and dates. Be ready to give a general explanation as to why you are requesting a meeting. That's all it takes.

Once you have the appointment with your elected official (or with the legislative aide, when lobbying a federal official), you need to focus on which issues you will discuss. Here are some ideas:

BILLS. Be specific as to your position on a pending piece of legislation by stating your opposition or support.

GENERAL ISSUES. Give your general feelings about a topic—some ideas include gun control, animal rights, the environment, child abuse, abortion rights, and welfare. Ask them to keep your views in mind when they vote on these issues.

FEEDBACK ON PAST VOTES. If a legislator voted against a bill you favored, discuss why he or she voted against it. Doing so might convince the official to vote differently in the future.

TIPS FOR A SUCCESSFUL MEETING

Be relaxed and calm during the meeting. This is your opportunity to express yourself. Many legislators enjoy this give-and-take with their constituents. It's a refreshing break from the daily schmoozing with trained lobbyists. Be honest, clear, and to the point about your feelings. Be forthright about your stand on a bill or issue; say right off the bat, "I support the Clean Water Act." Get your opinion heard loud and clear. Here are some other tips for a successful meeting.

DRESS APPROPRIATELY. Make sure you wear clean, nice-looking clothes.

BRING A FRIEND OR A GROUP OF FRIENDS. Having other concerned citizens with you will show there is additional support in the community. Be sure there is a general consensus as to what the meeting is about and that you are the main spokesperson. Without an appointed spokesperson, you run the risk of having chaos and misrepresentation at the meeting.

If you bring a group of people, be sure to send out a news release to the local media. Grassroots lobbying by private citizens might interest some journalists. If you plan on meeting your legislator at the main office in the capitol building, you can send out a statewide release in a few minutes. Your state capitol has a press office where journalists representing major newspapers and television and radio outlets receive daily news releases. The morning of your appointment, drop off fifty copies of your news release to inform every major media outlet of your lobbying efforts. It could lead to statewide exposure.

KEEP THE MEETING SHORT. No meeting should last longer than fifteen minutes. But if your legislator insists on ending the meeting in under five minutes, tell him or her that you deserve at least a few minutes of time. You did, after all, take time out of your busy schedule to meet with your elected official. You—and/or your friends and family— do vote.

BRING THE BILL WITH YOU. Some legislators might try to get out of taking a stand on a bill by saying they do not have a copy handy. Be thorough (and annoyingly efficient) by bringing two copies of the bill with you. (Use the resources mentioned earlier to get copies of the bill.)

USE GRAPHICS. Bring photographs or letters from people in the community supporting your efforts. For example, if you want to save a local forest from being logged, bring photos of the forest and supportive letters from voters in the district.

HAVE FUN AT THE MEETING. Be creative. Never threaten. Ask questions. Most important, stress the importance to you of your issue or your position on a bill.

AFTER THE MEETING

A few days after your meeting, send a thank-you note to your legislator. Mention you look forward to receiving his or her support for your issue and would appreciate any specific feedback on the actions their office took after your meeting. Leave a phone number and mailing address so the legislator's aide can contact you with an update.

OTHER WAYS TO GET YOUR VOICE HEARD LOUD AND CLEAR!

You don't have time to meet with your legislator? No problem. You can still get your opinion heard by devoting a few minutes every week to creating a friendly relationship with your legislator. This is not as powerful as a face-to-face meeting, but these ideas are still very effective in influencing the way your legislator votes.

MAKE A PHONE CALL. Ever call a company's 800 number to complain about a product? Do the same with your legislator and leave a constituent comment. A one-sentence comment like "I would like Senator Smith to support Bill Number 379, the Clean Air Law" is all an elected official needs to hear to keep track of who supports or opposes a bill in his district. Your one call could make the difference. Also, leave your name and address for a response from the legislator.

FAX OR MAIL A LETTER. Get this: Every time you send a letter to your legislator, it is believed your view equals that of ten other constituents in your district. Even more amazing: A letter to the president of the United States equals the same views of one hundred other U.S. citizens! Believe me, your letters really do count.

E-MAIL. Don't you love technology? Many of our elected officials are now on-line. You can check their Web sites to catch up on their voting record and leave comments at their e-mail addresses. Call the local district offices for their Web site and e-mail addresses. To get your e-mail campaign started, leave a message for the president of the United States at: president@whitehouse.gov or e-mail the vice president at: vicepresident@whitehouse.gov

Isn't lobbying easy? The process of influencing legislation on the local, state, and federal level is one every concerned citizen needs to understand and participate in. We have the power to make our opinions heard on issues we care about. By creating a positive, working relationship with your legislators, you can become a constant, influential force in their lives. Without your vote, they know they'll be out of a job come election time. Make your legislators aware of your beliefs, your needs, and your thoughts and hold them accountable for their actions.

TOOLS OF THE TRADE

Join Common Cause, a national, nonpartisan lobbying group working to bring people across the country together in an effort to lobby elected officials on issues of mutual concern. Some victories include winning passage of a comprehensive lobbying gift ban, lobby disclosure for legislators, and pressing for civil and equal rights for all citizens. For a free membership form, write: Common Cause, 2030 M Street, NW, Washington, DC 20036-3380; or call 202-833-1200.

Chapter Six

How to Organize an Event

W hen you think of a special event, what comes to mind? A celebrity gala? A political fund-raiser? A black-tie charity ball? How about church bingo night? A carnival? A beach cleanup? These are all special events. In fact, anything that brings a group of people together (including Aunt Edna's boring picnic last summer) is a special event.

In grassroots activism, the foundation of an effective organization is its ability to quickly and properly organize a special event. But if the thought of sending out invitations, recruiting volunteers, and making finger sandwiches for a hundred people frightens you, don't worry. Organizing a special event is easy to do when you start with clear goals and plan ahead.

THE PRODIGY OF PARTIES

I've learned a lot from organizing dozens of special events. In 1994, right after wrapping up my antidissection campaign, I decided to devote a few months to more upbeat and less controversial projects. I didn't want to read any more editorials criticizing my work. I wanted a rest from defending my ethics to what seemed like a never-ending jury of teachers, administrators, and reporters. I wanted to do something that wouldn't give me the teeth-grinding, eye-crossing headache the previous campaign did. A special event was the perfect solution.

On one of my regular visits to a nearby ecology store, I found the owner struggling to put together a neighborhood beautification event. Being a good friend and the self-proclaimed master of special event organizing, I decided to help out.

I sat down and made a list of goals for the event. I wanted the mayor of Reading, Pennsylvania, to attend, neighborhood children to show up in droves, the local media to cover it, and a handful of Earth 2000 members to help out. I also made a list of things that might hinder the success of the event—bad weather, poor turnout, and no money topped the list. I knew what I had and didn't have to work with, and was ready to organize the best event ever.

I sent invitations to the mayor's office; an invitation he eagerly accepted. News releases were faxed to local newspapers and television stations, and several made mention of the clean-up. I designed posters and distributed hundreds of them throughout the community; a few phone calls came in from the public eager to join us. I even took hundreds of helium-filled balloons from an art auction I attended the night before the cleanup and brought them to the event. The store owner handled everything else: buying the refreshments, providing the trash bags, and recruiting her neighbors.

The morning of the event, I showed up bright and early to set up the props, to arrange the refreshments, and to do anything else that needed to be done. I thought to myself how I was the master of special events, the whiz of organizing, the prodigy of parties. Then the sky turned gray.

With forty people—including the mayor, small children, and members of Earth 2000—coming in less than half an hour, I was worried rain would spoil what I had proclaimed an "absolutely perfect" event. As I nervously watched the sky I was totally unaware that the event itself would give me one of those teeth-grinding, eye-crossing headaches.

I had to corral impatient, misbehaving children and keep them from running onto private property. I rudely yelled at Earth 2000 members for being "unreasonably late" (actually only five minutes). I didn't purchase enough work gloves, and the gloves I did buy were of poor quality, quickly falling apart when coming in contact with water. I wrestled hypodermic needles away from the bare hands of small children, while trying my best to keep the mayor from seeing all the signs of drug use in that area (he saw them anyway). Even the scissors the mayor used to cut through the ceremonial ribbon failed to work, and I had to tear the ribbon with my teeth. To top it all off, a bag of garbage—most of it containing used diapers and half-empty beer bottles—ripped open all over my pants and shoes. At the end of the day, with my head pounding and my feet aching, I knew some powerful force was out to prove me wrong: I'm no whiz at organizing special events.

Well, I did learn my lesson. With my feet and ego firmly planted on the ground, I've learned to relax and to treat special events with a proper mix of discipline and fun. With enough practice over the years—from organizing field trips for children to hosting murder mystery fund-raisers—I've actually gotten quite good at planning events. I can buy airline tickets with ease (at bargain basement prices), whip up a last-minute dinner party for unexpected guests, and even get free tickets to a high-profile gala in Washington, D.C. But with the special event debacle of 1994 still fresh in my mind (and my occasional nightmare), I will never, ever again call myself the master of special events.

DECK THE HALLS

If you can avoid proclaiming yourself the prodigy of parties, I recommend you try putting special events into your activist repertoire. I will not be outlining the tools and resources needed to organize a celebrity party or high-profile fashion show; odds are you will not be doing one of these star-studded events in the near future. I will, however, give examples of several types of easy-to-replicate, small-scale special events that will raise awareness of your cause and pride in your community. I tell you *who* you should contact, *when* to start organizing, and *what* are the absolute must-do's. And remember, don't let the hard work associated with organizing special events overwhelm you. Try to have fun, too!

OUTDOOR EVENTS

Oh, the great outdoors with its babbling brooks and chirping birds. What a shame we spend so much time indoors, at shopping malls, in office buildings, at home, and locked in our cars. Sad, isn't it? It doesn't have to be. Organize an *outdoor* special event and introduce people to the lush grass, towering trees, and soft sand of the great outdoors.

PICNICS. Whether to celebrate a campaign win or to bring people together for new member orientation, a picnic is a great outdoor event. All you need is some food, a few drinks, and a little music. But remember, it's not just a party. The event should have a purpose. Take a few minutes during the event to talk about future campaigns and to congratulate any members who are doing an outstanding job.

Who: Contact the park manager and ask about permit requirements for your picnic; you may not need one. Also, send invitations to guests.

When: Contact everyone about the picnic at least a month ahead of time. Make sure they RSVP!

What: Bring food. Try to receive in-kind donations of food from local grocers and bakers. Be careful about alcohol; there might be an "open bottle" law in your community. Call City Hall to find out.

CLEANUPS. Environmentalists aren't the only ones doing cleanups. Everyone is pitching in today to pick up litter from beaches, forests, and highways. Cleanups bond people together for one simple reason: They can see an immediate improvement. If you don't organize one for conservation reasons, do one for the team-building effects.

Who: Contact members and volunteers. Also, contact the city sanitation department so they can pick up your filled trash bags when you're finished.

When: Invitations to the event should be sent at least three weeks ahead of time. RSVP, if possible.

What: Bring gloves, trash bags, a first-aid kit, and plenty of bottled water.

WALKATHONS. These are events where individuals receive donations from friends, coworkers, and neighbors for every mile they walk. All money raised is given to the charity organizing the event. I do not recommend you organize a walkathon; they are very difficult to put together. Instead, gather some friends and walk as a group in an existing walkathon. TIP: Be sure the monies go to a charity whose philosophy you agree with. For example, I stopped walking in the March of Dimes Walk America because I discovered the money went to fund experiments on kittens, something I strongly oppose.

Who: Contact your friends, family, and members.

When: Contact everyone as soon as you receive information about the walkathon.

What: Be sure to register everyone for the event and distribute the pledge forms to them early so they, too, can collect pledges.

FOR THE INTELLECTUAL

What do you like to think about? World politics? Chernobyl? Peace in the Middle East? Organize a special event to create a brainstorm of independent thoughts and ideas. Who knows? Maybe some Sunday afternoon you'll come up with a solution to world hunger.

WORKSHOPS. Invite a specialist in your field of interest to present a workshop. Executives from nonprofits, renowned activists, and public relations consultants are great workshop speakers. These are terrific opportunities to train members in activism skills. A college is a great place to host a workshop.

Who: Ask a local prominent expert like an author or

activist in your field to present a talk in a workshop. Check the local newspaper for human-interest stories of people in your field; they might also be interested in being a presenter.

When: Book a presenter three months ahead of time. Contact a local college or university as soon as possible about reserving a room. Send out notices two months ahead of time to ten times the number of people you can accommodate (for example, if you want fifty people to attend, send out five hundred invitations).

What: Make sure you have enough people attending the workshop. If not, be smart and cancel the entire program out of respect for the presenter. Providing coffee and snack foods keeps people happy.

BOOK DISCUSSIONS. On a cold Thursday night, a group of six people sit around a roaring fire sipping Blue Mountain Jamaican coffee, discussing a new political biography. Sound nice? Choose a topic-oriented book (the more controversial the better) to discuss with interested members and the public. A bookstore is a great location for this event.

Who: Contact the manager of the bookstore to co-organize the event. The store can offer a special price on the chosen book to encourage people to purchase it. Post signs in the store inviting shoppers to attend the discussion.

When: Make your initial contact at least two months ahead of time.

What: Draw people to the discussion by offering free coffee, some snacks, and maybe a few door prizes. Send a news release to the local media, too. If the author lives nearby, send an invitation to him or her to attend and participate in the discussion.

SPEAKERS. Inviting successful activists and well-known personalities to speak to an audience is a great way to painlessly inspire people. Also, the general public can attend a presentation and not feel pressured to participate. It's also a positive way to introduce people to new ideas. A college auditorium is a good place for a speech presentation.

Who: Contact the speaker or their assistant. For well-known presenters like Jane Goodall, you may need to place a booking at least a year ahead of time *and* pay an honorarium of up to $20,000. Too much? Try to get someone to do it for free, or if you have some funds, contact a speakers bureau to place a booking for a less-expensive speaker. Contact the college after booking the speaker.

When: Book a presenter three to five months ahead of time. Invite the public to attend by conducting a PR blitz. Send out news releases, do television appearances, conduct radio interviews, and post signs in high-traffic areas. The college communications office can also help with media relations. Do all of this at least two months ahead of time.

What: Make sure the speaker's miscellaneous arrangements are taken care of, like travel to and from the airport, housing, and meals.

FIELD TRIPS. Take a trip to your state capitol or the U.S. Congress for a day of lobbying. By handling the travel and schedule for novice activists, you can make their first lobbying experience fulfilling and easy.

Who: Contact your members and interested non-members to determine how many people will be attending. Either reserve a bus or minivan through a travel agent (it'll cost from $100 to $500, depending on the size and traveling time) or organize a car pool among participants. If you decide to charter a bus, be sure the costs are evenly divided among the participants (e.g., $300 for the bus divided by thirty participants equals $10 apiece). Also, schedule meetings with three legislators for that day.

When: Contact your members at least a month ahead of time. Once you've figured out how many people are attending, make the final travel arrangements. Contact legislator's aides at least three weeks ahead of time.

What: Make sure everyone dresses appropriately and is well informed about the legislative issues you'll be discussing.

SCHOOL EVENTS

Schools, being strapped for cash, are always appreciative of help from campus-based groups. Your show of generosity is an opportunity to influence, educate, and enlighten the minds of your apathetic peers. These events are great for parental participation. Here are some of my favorites.

ASSEMBLIES. Bring in interesting speakers, touring groups, or educational movies for the student body. You can ask a like-minded national organization's director of education for a list of suggestions. But remember this tip in planning: The program should be tailored to the audience's comprehension level (e.g., a screening of *Schindler's List* for a third-grade class is probably not appropriate).

Who: Contact the student council adviser or the high school principal. Also, contact the person in charge of booking your presenter.

When: Make your initial contact with the school at least a month before the start of the new school year so as to be included in that year's schedule. Book the presenter immediately after receiving approval from the school.

What: Be sure to have information—promotional flyers, press kits, and background information about your assembly—to present to the school. And do not charge the school for the assembly; they don't have the funds.

CONTESTS. Who doesn't love a good competition? Organize a poster or essay contest focused around your cause. Offer a small prize—a trophy or gift certificate—for the winning entry. Be sure to send out a news release to the local newspaper to recognize the winner and other competitors. This is a great event for young kids.

Who: Contact the school's principal. Ask him or her to spread the word about the contest through the school mail system and over the public address system.

When: Make the initial contact at least a month before the start of the contest.

What: Be specific on the theme of the contest. For example, instead of using "the environment" as a theme, consider something like "the endangered Florida everglades." The less confusion the better.

DANCES. Offer to sponsor the next school dance. The dance's theme should reflect your cause (e.g., A Night in the Rain Forest). Use plenty of literature and posters to stress the theme. And since the dance is already a regular weekly or monthly event, you don't need to market the dance or book the school's gym; it's already done.

Who: Contact the dance coordinator, usually the student government adviser.

When: Contact the coordinator at least two months prior to your target date.

What: Be clear about your theme from the start. Also, consider placing a donation jar at the entrance for students to give a few dollars to a charity connected with the theme.

FIELD TRIPS. Invite a class to take an educational outing. State parks, farms, food factories, and power plants are a few places kids enjoy visiting. Because youngsters have short attention spans, try to choose a place that teaches kids about your cause while entertaining them.

Who: Contact the classroom teacher. Upon agreement, the teacher can handle the permission forms and paperwork to clear the trip with the school and parents.

When: Contact the teacher at least three months prior to your ideal field trip date. Be sure to consider the weather. Don't plan a field trip during the winter months; it might snow.

What: Make sure you have absolute permission to bring a group of kids to your field trip site. Get it in writing. Also, make sure the teacher remembers to order a bus for that day.

HANDS-ON PROJECTS. Great for younger kids. Co-organize a "hands-on" activity with students in grades K–5 to educate them about your issue. High school students could discuss the benefits of living a drug-free lifestyle by serving as role models for these younger kids. Use arts and craft supplies to make it a truly hands-on project. Be creative and make it fun.

Who: Contact the teacher or school principal.

When: Make the initial contact at least two months prior to the desired date.

What: Provide all of the supplies and materials. If you need photocopies, make them ahead of time. Come prepared; the teacher will thank you.

FUND-RAISING EVENTS

I don't believe in organizing special events for the sole purpose of raising funds. Instead, incorporate fund-raising into a special event to, as the saying goes, kill two birds with one stone. (By the way, I certainly don't advocate killing *any* birds.)

Any of these fund-raising ideas can be used in conjunction with any of the above special events. I do not, however, recommend incorporating fund-raising into a school event. That would be tacky.

PLEDGE CARDS. Leave pledge cards—an index-size card that allows people to pledge a donation to your group—around the event site. They will encourage people to commit a small amount to your organization. Potential funds raised: $100 to $300.

ATTENDANCE FEES. Leave a donation box at the entrance to the workshop or speaker's presentation for people to leave a contribution. Ask a $1 to $3 freewill donation. If people feel uncomfortable donating, they don't have to. Potential funds raised: $100 to $500.

DONATION BOX. Leave a donation jar by the refreshments table. When people help themselves to coffee and doughnuts, they're likely to leave a donation just because it's the courteous thing to do. Potential funds raised: $50 to $100.

RAFFLE. Sell tickets during the event to raffle off a prize donated by a local business. Airline tickets, electronics, and gift baskets are great prizes. Sell individual tickets for $2, three for $5. Pick the winner at the end of the event. Potential funds raised: $100 to $600.

SELL BOOKS. If the speaker is an author, purchase copies of the book in bulk from the publisher. Sell the autographed copies at the cover price to the audience. Guaranteed sellout! Potential funds raised: $100 to $400.

AFTER IT'S OVER

Conduct a survey at the conclusion of your event to determine participants' overall satisfaction level. It is critical that you receive feedback. These opinions can be used to improve events in the future.

Randomly choose a few participants to fill out surveys on which you ask for general ideas and input. Also, ask for their ratings on specific aspects. For example, a good question for a workshop might be: On a scale of 1–10 (1 being the worst, 10 being the best), how would you rate the question-and-answer session of the workshop?

While the concept of special events hasn't changed over the years, the notion that they're hard to put together has. They're not. Try organizing one, and remember: Practice makes perfect.

Chapter Seven

McFight
McCorporate
Abuse—Boycott!

Corporate America is everywhere. Tune in to any special event on television; they all have at least one corporate sponsor. The U.S. Open (golf and tennis), the Superbowl, and especially the Centennial Olympic Games in Atlanta—they all have dozens or even hundreds of corporate sponsors.

The barrage of advertising all over the world is so overwhelming that a Vancouver-based organization called The Media Foundation coordinates a Buy Nothing Day on November 29 to, as the name suggests, encourage people not to spend money. But word of the event hasn't reached the mainstream folks yet. The top networks—ABC, CBS, and NBC—refuse to run the group's Buy

Nothing commercials, or as the foundation calls them "uncommercials," even though the foundation is willing to pay for the spots. Networks fear losing sponsors if they run the anticorporation ads.

But the most upsetting feature of Corporate America to me is their exploitation of the environment, of animals, and of human beings for the sake of profit. Entire forests are clear-cut, millions of animals are tortured in laboratories, and human beings work in sweatshops to make the bottom line bigger. I call it Corporate Gluttony.

McDOMINATION

Get this. On June 28, 1994, the giant McDonald's fast-food chain filed a civil lawsuit against two London environmental activists for distributing an anti-McDonald's flyer called "What's Wrong with McDonald's." The factsheet stated that McDonald's sold high-fat, high-sodium food that could lead to heart disease; exploited children through the use of advertising and gimmicks; and cruelly raised animals for slaughter.

The multibillion-dollar corporation had actually begun its campaign against the activists five years earlier, when the company hired four spies to infiltrate the tiny London grassroots organization in hopes of gathering information about their activities. McDonald's spent millions of dollars to silence even the smallest of critics. Scary.

Unfortunately, corporations all over the world are guilty of being Corporate Gluttons. Environmental disasters like the *Exxon Valdez* and Mitsubishi rain forest clearcuts are just two infamous examples.

DEPRESSED YET?

Don't be. There are a number of things you, as a concerned consumer, can do to stop Corporate Gluttony. Specifically, you can launch a consumer boycott.

I believe the most powerful tools of the American citizen are the power to vote and the power to decide which goods and services to purchase. With so many corporations in competition for your money, you have the power to speak up against corporate abuse by refusing to patronize a particular business. No matter how many commercials, celebrity spokespeople, and free samples a corporation may tempt you with, they shouldn't receive a dime from you if you disagree with their policies. With more and more American consumers refusing to purchase certain brands or products in hopes of effecting some corporate change, boycotts are becoming a popular way for individuals to express their views.

To successfully change a corporation, hundreds—if not thousands—of people need to boycott collectively. To recruit people into your campaign, you need to start a chain reaction. Have your friends and family join the boycott effort. Then ask them to each tell two more people, who tell two people, who tell two people, and so on. When others see people taking action against a corporation, they'll want to take a stand, too. A boycott, after all, is simply an organized method of communicating complaints to the company. Pretty soon, a corporation will feel these comments in the pocketbook and will change their policy to regain lost business.

LERNER LEARNS A LESSON

I launched my most successful boycott campaign in 1995. And it convinced me that boycotts really do work.

It all started when I accompanied my friend Jennell to a Lerner New York store so she could return a pair of jeans. While waiting with her in the very long return line, I familiarized myself with the surroundings. I complained to Jennell about the tacky pink, brown, and lime green wall coverings. I remarked on how overcommercialized the sitcom "Friends" had become; they were on T-shirts, posters, and keychains throughout the store. And I even whined about missing the movie I so badly wanted to see, as this "It'll only take five minutes" trip edged to the one-hour mark.

As time slowly passed, I became increasingly less patient and more critical of tiny, insignificant problems. "It's too hot. It's too cold. I'm hungry. I'm sick," I complained. And being such a "pain" (as Jennell put it), perhaps I was a bit too moody, angry, and agitated to handle problems, especially those of real significance. So what happened next is understandable.

I noticed *real* fur–trimmed coats for sale in the corner of the store. Next to the orange leopard jackets and purple/green gingham stretch pants, were shiny silver and gold anorak jackets with white fur trim. I was outraged. Being an animal rights activist with a personal passion to rid the world of fur coats, I yelled across the store, "Boycott Lerner! Fur is murder!" over and over again. I motioned to Jennell to leave the store with me at the same moment it was her turn in line. So when she finished exchanging her jeans, Jennell quickly ran out of Lerner New York, too embarrassed to be seen with me. I, on the other hand, was still chanting in my one-man protest.

I stormed home and called the Lerner New York corporate offices demanding a response to my antifur sentiments. A spokesperson read to me from a form letter that stated: "Our concerns tend to be more concentrated on fashion elements than animal rights issues." She hung up, and I was furious.

From 5:00 P.M. until 3:00 A.M., I licked, stuffed, sealed, and addressed fifteen hundred envelopes containing action alerts to Earth 2000 members. I wrote a press release with headline reading "Teen Consumers Fight Back: Lerner New York Is a Fur Faux Pas" and faxed it to two hundred media outlets using my computer media data base. In less than twenty-four hours I launched the Boycott Lerner New York campaign.

Over the course of several weeks, Earth 2000 members wrote letters to Lerner. They recruited friends, family, and strangers to join the campaign. They convinced their parents to tear up Lerner charge cards and return them to the company president via certified mail. They even shipped old Lerner clothing to the corporate headquarters demanding a refund. Thousands of people reacted to my rapid-response boycott campaign.

Today, Lerner New York no longer uses fur. After receiving ten thousand letters from consumers supporting the boycott and hundreds of Lerner charge cards, they decided the consumer proved there was a real lack of demand for fur products. By recruiting teenagers who also recruited their parents, I proved my theory that teens had consumer clout. And when 834 Lerner New York stores declared themselves fur-free shopping zones in 1996, I learned the power consumers have when they join together to fight corporate abuse. Boycotts work.

SAMPLE BOYCOTTS

Not all boycotts are animal rights related. Here are some boycotts announced in the fall 1995 issue of *Boycott Quarterly* (a great source for information about ongoing boycotts; see "Tools of the Trade"). As you can see, boycotts are launched by a diverse number of organizations, for a diverse number of reasons, against a diverse group of corporations.

BLOCKBUSTER VIDEO BOYCOTT. Blockbuster is charged with practicing censorship by refusing to carry videos that company executives deem offensive. Boycott called by: Californians Against Censorship Together, and Fred Moore's Chero Company.

KMART BOYCOTT. Kmart, through its subsidiary Waldenbooks, is one of the leading retailers of pornography in the United States. Boycott called by: American Family Association.

PIZZA HUT BOYCOTT. Pizza Hut is using Rush Limbaugh as a spokesperson in its television advertising. Organizers charge Limbaugh with "hate mongering." Boycott called by: Silicon Valley Clinton/Gore Democratic Club.

Nonprofit groups also launch boycott campaigns against other nonprofit groups:

THE NATURE CONSERVANCY (TNC) BOYCOTT. TNC is using unnecessarily cruel means to remove feral pigs, goats, and other animals from its lands in the Hawaiian Islands and elsewhere. Boycott called by: People for the Ethical Treatment of Animals.

DO BOYCOTTS *REALLY* WORK?

I believe consumer boycott campaigns are the most effective way to spark corporate reform. The animal rights movement has known this for years and forced Corporate America to make changes in the way it does business. People for the Ethical Treatment of Animals (PETA), the world's largest animal rights organization, is responsible for forcing Benetton, Revlon, L'Oréal, and a host of other major corporations to abandon their animal-testing policies and find nonanimal alternatives. PETA's members were persistent in boycotting animal-tested cosmetics and wrote thousands of letters to boycotted corporations to express their animal rights views; no corporation could ignore sacks of angry letters and sinking profit margins. But PETA's effects went far beyond changing one corporation's policy.

Because so many consumers demanded that their toiletries and cosmetics not be tested on animals, the beauty industry decided to turn this public relations lemon into lemonade. They invented "cruelty free" products for this new market of conscious consumers. For example, The Body Shop's slogan, "Against Animal Testing," can be seen boldly printed on their products, on giant signs in the stores, and on T-shirts worn by company employees. They sided with the animal rightists and, in the process, made millions of dollars reaping the benefits of being the "good guy" in the industry. Today, very few cosmetic corporations want the negative image that comes with animal testing.

The same can be said for the fur industry. PETA fought the barbaric fur industry by recruiting supermodels and stars Christy Turlington, Joel West, Cindy Crawford,

Melissa Etheridge, and Kim Basinger to pose nude for their "I'd rather go naked than wear fur" campaign. This, in my opinion, was a brilliant consumer boycott. This campaign, in addition to exposing the cruelty in wearing fur, took the glamour out of wearing fur. Top designers Calvin Klein and Donna Karan stopped selling fur coats because of consumer pressures directly accredited to PETA. Even the general public ate it up: In a recent Associated Press poll, more than 80 percent of Americans believed it was absolutely wrong to skin an animal for its fur. Thanks in part to PETA, consumers stopped associating fur with glamour; instead, the industry was perceived as a cold-hearted, greedy business—an image, in my opinion, it wholeheartedly deserves.

SO, HOW DO I START A CONSUMER BOYCOTT CAMPAIGN?

You read the morning newspaper only to discover a department store chain has announced plans to sell Rush Limbaugh's line of ties. Bad news. It angers you so much that you phone the company's corporate headquarters and leave a colorful comment with an uninterested secretary. You think to yourself, Now what?

Before launching an all-out boycott effort, try single-handedly raising hell. Sometimes even one person can force a company to change. When I was thirteen years old, I was upset to see a live lobster being thrown onto the floor and smashed to pieces on the TV game show "Supermarket Sweep." I wrote a letter to the producer of the show, telling him to remove the live lobsters or I would stop watching the show. In a few days, the producer agreed to my request.

I won! I didn't have to launch a viewer boycott or spend more than the price of a stamp on the effort.

YOUR FIRST STEPS

Find out the name of the chief executive officer or chairman of the corporation. Also, get the mailing address of the corporate headquarters where the head honcho works.

Type or neatly handwrite a one-page letter to the CEO or chairman explaining that you are a devoted customer and feel their plans are inappropriate. Explain how you—and your friends and family—go out of your way to avoid stores that endorse Rush Limbaugh's politics. Be clear that you will no longer shop there if they continue. If you have a store credit card, cut it up and include it with your letter. Use the sample letter on page 108 as a guide. Be specific—never, ever vulgar!—in your letter.

TIP: Send the letter via certified mail to ensure they receive it.

If you don't receive a response after one week, call the corporate headquarters *every single day* until you get a response to your letter. Your goal is to annoy them as much as possible. The more persistent you are, the more likely you'll get someone's attention.

THEY DON'T CARE

Some corporate heads will ignore your letters and calls. Do what I do: Send one hundred identical letters (yes, one hundred!) to the attention of the corporate head. Send these letters all at the same time. I don't know anyone

Mr. Timothy Grumbacher, President
The Bon-Ton Corporate Offices
P.O. Box 2821
York, PA 17405

March 19, 1996

Dear Mr. Grumbacher:

I was upset to read in this morning's newspaper about your corporation's plans to lease space to Pollack Furs. As a longtime Bon-Ton patron, I am extremely displeased about your decision to allow fur coats in your stores.

As stated in the *Reading Eagle/Times* article, Pollack Furs president Robert Pollack stated that it was your corporation's desire to "upgrade the merchandise Bon-Ton carries in its stores." Clearly, the fashion community has overwhelmingly rejected fur, with leading designers Calvin Klein, Donna Karan, and Giorgio Armani refusing to use real fur. I hope that Bon-Ton will follow in those footsteps.

Until you decide to make that compassionate step, I—and my friends and family—will no longer shop at Bon-Ton. Enclosed is my cut-up Bon-Ton charge card. Mr. Grumbacher, fur has no place in a modern, humane society. Listen to your consumers and ban fur now.

Regards,

Danny Seo
Green Hills, PA

important enough not to notice your persistence, with maybe the exception of the president, the pope, and Madonna.

If they refuse to drop their plans, it's time to launch a consumer boycott campaign.

HOW TO START A CONSUMER BOYCOTT CAMPAIGN

When I launched a boycott campaign against Bon-Ton Department Stores for planning to open two fur salons, I wanted every consumer in Bon-Ton's main shopping districts to know about it. I did this by sending Action Alerts to members of Earth 2000 and by notifying the media of my efforts.

An "action alert" is exactly what it sounds like: It alerts people to an action you want them to take. Your action alert should include an address, the name of a contact person, and the fax and phone numbers for the boycotted corporation in addition to the reasons for the boycott. Check out the sample action alert on page 110 for ideas. This one was used for my campaign against Bon-Ton Department Stores. To save money, design an action alert that can be mailed like a postcard—the postage rate and overall printing cost will be much lower. Send it to your members, your volunteers, and anyone else you think will give a damn about your campaign. Leave some where people will pick them up, including coffeehouses, supermarkets, and schools. TIP: Remind people to not only boycott the corporation but to send a note to the company, explaining why they are boycotting.

Next, use the media skills in Chapter 3 to notify the local media about your efforts. Because boycott campaigns

Action Alert

Fur Salons Planned for Bon-Ton Department Stores!
Urgent Action Needed!

The Reading, PA-based Pollack Furs has recently announced plans to open up fur salons in two Bon-Ton stores. Pollack Furs president Robert Pollack said the move is to "upgrade the merchandise Bon-Ton carries in its stores." The salons are expected to open in September.

According to recent news clippings, Pollack Furs plans to bring fur-clad fashion through the entire Bon-Ton chain of 70 stores, too.

Earth 2000 National has sent an official letter of objection via certified mail to Bon-Ton's president. Here's how you can help:

1. Send a letter denouncing Bon-Ton's pro-fur agreement.
2. Cut up your Bon-Ton charge card and include it with your letter.

Be sure to mention that top designers Calvin Klein and Donna Karan refuse to design with fur. Also, mention your friends and family will boycott Bon-Ton until the fur scam ceases.

Send your protest letter and destroyed Bon-Ton charge card to:

Mr. Timothy Grumbacher, President
The Bon-Ton Corporate Offices
P.O. Box 2821
York, PA 17405

are nothing new to the media, you need to make your story fresh and interesting. If you're a young person, use a headline in your news release like "Teenager vs. XYZ Corporation." In my efforts against Bon-Ton, newspaper headlines read "Teen Activist vs. Bon-Ton." If you're an older individual, use a headline like "Moms Take On XYZ Corporation" or "Seniors Angry Over XYZ's Plans." Your goal is to give your story an edge by bringing your trail-blazing grassroots campaign to the attention of the editors.

Here's a surprise tip: Fax your action alerts and news releases to the corporation you are boycotting. If they see you are taking serious, hard-core action against them, it may be enough to convince them to change their plans. In their eyes, a boycott is like a cancerous growth in the body that just won't go away. Except, in this case, a cure is available: They can concede to your demands.

MAKING *THEM* PAY FOR YOUR CAMPAIGN

Because there is so much competition among similar corporations, many businesses offer toll-free and postage-paid outlets for consumers to offer suggestions on how the corporation can improve its goods and services. It's called relationship marketing. You can express your outrage at *their* expense. Some of these outlets include:

800 COMMENT LINES Call 800-555-1212 (toll-free) and ask the operator if the corporation has an 800 phone number. Distribute this phone number to as many people as possible—especially those out of state—and ask them to call and leave a complaint. The corporation pays for these calls; it's free for you to call as many times as you like.

COMMENT CARDS. Many retail corporations have postage-paid comment cards dispersed throughout their stores for shoppers to use to evaluate the store's goods and services. You can fill them out and mail them—no postage necessary! The corporation pays a high premium to the postal service for this business-reply service. There is no limit to the number of cards you can fill out; they are, after all, free.

CREDIT CARD APPLICATIONS. There's a credit card for everyone today. From the General Motors MasterCard to the Bloomingdale's gold charge card, every company is jumping onto the credit card bandwagon. If store credit card applications are readily available, use them as comment cards instead. Mail as many as you like with your feelings about the corporation. When animal rights activists boycotted American Express (AmEx) for selling fur coats in its catalog, activists simply wrote "Fur is dead" on AmEx postage-paid application forms. Many filled out hundreds of them until the company agreed to stop selling fur.

CATALOGS. If you receive a catalog from a boycotted company, send it back at the company's expense. Write "return to sender" and circle the return address. Be sure to leave your comments on the catalog cover for them to read. The company pays for postage; you get your message heard.

Given the diversity among corporations, each boycott effort must be coordinated individually. I've presented just a grab bag of tactical tools. These skills and ideas can serve as your blueprint. Build a campaign from these plans and kick some corporate butt!

We must hold corporations accountable for their destructive actions. By making wise and intelligent choices in our shopping, we cast important "votes" in favor of corporations who do business in a socially responsible manner. We may be viewed as kooks, radicals, or hippies, but name-calling won't stop us. It is our responsibility as consumers to speak out against corporate abuse by taking a stand. And with boycotts, we will.

TOOLS OF THE TRADE

• Subscribe to *Adbusters Quarterly*, a journal of ad parodies designed to provoke thought about the culture of advertising. Contact: The Media Foundation, 1243 West 7th Avenue, Vancouver, BC Canada. Visit their amusing Web site: http://hoshi.cic.sfu.ca/adbusters

• Read *Shopping for a Better World* by the Council on Economic Priorities (New York: Ballantine, 1993). It grades popular consumer goods on issues ranging from environmental protection to women's issues.

• Join the Center for the Study of Commercialism (CSC). This national organization works to "turn a nation of TV-watching consumers into a nation of concerned, involved citizens." Write: CSC, 1875 Connecticut Avenue, NW, Suite 300, Washington, DC 20009-5728.

• Subscribe to *Boycott Quarterly*. Printed four times a year, this magazine lists new and ongoing boycott efforts launched by such diverse groups as the Catholic League and the International Campaign for Tibet. A fascinating publication. Write: P.O. Box 30727, Seattle, WA 98103-0727.

• Visit your local library and check out the September/October 1993 issue of *Utne Reader*. The cover story, "Let Them Eat Rainforest Crunch," explores the question: Does Socially Responsible Business Really Make a Difference? You decide.

Chapter Eight

Hey, Hey . . . Ho, Ho . . . We're Not Going to Take It Anymore

There are many forms of protest: verbal, physical, and even electronic. Chances are you've seen one or all of these types in action. Perhaps you've witnessed a large group of people holding signs outside an office building screaming catchy slogans through bullhorns. Maybe you know someone who has chained himself to the entrance of an abortion clinic being arrested and seen by *everyone* on CNN and in *USA Today*. How about your quiet neighbor Mrs. Jones (you know, the one who *loves* "Matlock"), who regularly e-mails comments to elected officials and corporate CEOs? She is protesting through the Information Superhighway.

Everyone has his or her own definition of a protest. But

perhaps the most common preconceived notion about protests is that they are illegal activities in which everyone, sooner or later, is arrested.

This is not the case. The tiniest minority of protest activities will ever result in arrests. Because so much media attention is given to extreme, illegal protests (e.g., pouring blood into the White House water fountain) and nominal coverage to legal, peaceful protests, people automatically believe their presence at a protest will mean a night in the city slammer. Wrong. In the hundreds of protests I have coordinated and attended, I have never been arrested. In my opinion, a person has a better chance of being arrested for jaywalking than for attending a protest rally.

SAVE THE WHALES

The most successful protest I ever organized was in 1993 in Washington, D.C. It all began several years ago, when I started noticing an alarming number of stories about whales and dolphins being killed. I watched TV documentaries and read feature articles about marine mammals being slaughtered for human consumption in Asia and Europe. I was horrified at pictures in magazines of humans harpooning and cutting up the bodies of lifeless whales. But what could I—a fifteen-year-old student—do to stop the killings?

On a cold Friday night, with a cup of tea in one hand and the remote control in the other, I plopped my flu-stricken body in front of the television. I thought to myself, Good ol' TV. You'll make me feel better! I decided to watch "20/20."

Lynn Sherr was reporting on a controversy in a small

island colony near the North Atlantic called the Faeroe Islands. The islanders were in the middle of a dispute with environmentalists over their annual killing of pilot whales. The inhabitants of these islands, who kill more than two thousand pilot whales every year, said the whales provided needed food. But with a thriving seafood-export industry providing income to the citizens, in addition to the millions of dollars in economic subsidies they receive from the Danish government, the Faeroe Islands have one of the world's highest standards of living.

Expensive sports cars, cellular phones, well-stocked kitchens, and top-of-the-line electronic goods are all staples of the typical Faeroese family. How could such a rich people "need" to kill whales for food? Animal rights and environmental activists argued that the hunt was no longer a traditional harvest of whale meat but a rich man's killing sport.

I agreed. No modern, civilized society should kill whales. The Faeroe Islands, in my opinion, were using tradition as a smokescreen to defend their whaling practices. Outraged—and perhaps overly influenced by the cold medicine—I decided to organize a major protest against the Faeroe Islands whale kill.

By Monday morning I was coordinating a Washington, D.C., antiwhaling protest march. Because the Faeroe Islands did not have an embassy in the United States, my goal for the protest was to express my disapproval of Denmark's continued payment of economic subsidies to these islands. I named the campaign The War on Pilot Whales in the Faeroe Islands.

In between classes, I chartered a bus through my travel agent, called the U.S. Parks Department to obtain permits, worked on a national news release, invited students to attend the protest, and answered questions from a State

Department representative. All of this work naturally caused me to miss a few classes, to the disappointment of the high school principal. When I was questioned for being truant, I explained that my interview with the State Department could not be postponed. I was, after all, considered a potential "international threat" to the country of Denmark and therefore could not attend English or physical education classes.

On March 20, 1993—after two months of intense coordinating—I boarded a bus with other concerned Americans and headed to the nation's capital to let the world know how we felt about the Faeroese "tradition."

When the State Department sees individuals taking a stand against a foreign country, it is their job to investigate. Perhaps that's why officials greeted us at the entrance to the Danish embassy to take photos, to interview protesters, and to collect samples of flyers handed out during the protest. They were also there to get information about me. By the age of sixteen, I had a file with the State Department because I had the potential to threaten relations between the United States and Denmark. I couldn't drive a car, buy a pack of cigarettes, or drink a beer, but I *did* have the potential to cause problems between two countries. Go figure.

A line of police officers greeted us by creating a human wall around the embassy building. Even though we had no intention of entering the embassy grounds, a plan was devised to keep us away just in case. It was hard to figure out why the State Department investigators and police made such a huge commotion over a group of teenagers holding signs reading "Free the Whales" and carrying giant inflatable dolphins.

Reporters from European press bureaus attended the

event. In an article that ran in Copenhagen, Denmark, the next morning, a reporter wrote about the efforts of one determined teenager who made his antiwhaling message heard across the Atlantic Ocean. This article, in addition to hundreds that ran in the United States, Japan, and Europe, fueled an international boycott of Danish goods, pressuring Denmark to stop giving economic subsidies to the Faeroe Islands. According to the U.K. organization that announced the boycott, "It couldn't have been done without the demanding voices of a few determined teenagers in the States."

Since governments wouldn't take action against the whale hunts, I believed concerned citizens must. And I learned that a single voice could be heard across the Atlantic Ocean. Did the Danish government hear my cries of protest? Definitely. Was I a threat to the "tradition" of killing pilot whales? That, too.

Now, more than three years later, my campaign efforts are still of interest to the media. On the nationally televised "Pat Bullard Show" I was recently interviewed with Olympic gymnast Dominique Dawes and a kid hero who stopped a runaway bus. The host introduced me as, "the kid who has made such a big difference in the world that the State Department investigated him as a possible international threat."

SHOULD I ORGANIZE A PROTEST?

Protests should be organized only as a last resort. And that means only after you've tried every activist tactic possible—boycotts, letter-writing campaigns, and media appearances—should you consider a protest to finally convince an opposing force to change. Here's a good example of what I mean.

Remember the Boston Tea Party? In 1773, a historic action against British "taxation without representation" was organized by a group called the Sons of Liberty to protest a tax on tea. Americans successfully boycotted tea in Philadelphia, New York, and Charleston. The governor of Boston, however, upheld the tax and refused to allow the tea ships to leave port without paying. *As a last resort*, the Sons of Liberty boarded the ships, disguised as Indians, and dumped 342 chests of tea into the water. This particular protest was one of the events that led to the American Revolution and changed the course of the Colonies forever.

Okay, okay—the last thing you want to do is cause a revolution. I bet you also don't want to wear funny costumes and cause damage to private property. But many of you do want your protest to be heard, to be acknowledged, and to change someone's behavior. And if you're like most people, you don't know how to organize a protest. So, before you start painting signs and banners, you should learn a little more about the world of protests.

PLENTY OF PROTESTS TO PICK

PHYSICAL PROTESTS. These are demonstrations where people gather to picket outside an office building, event, or place of business. Protesters use signs, banners, chants, and even weird outfits to get attention from the public and media. These protests are legal when local authorities are notified and all of the necessary permits (if any) are obtained ahead of time (see page 122, "Permits," for information). No one is arrested if everyone abides by the town's "public gathering" policy.

BANNER DROPPING. When volunteer numbers are low, a banner dropping may be right for you. It is exactly what it sounds like: A giant banner is hung from a busy place where motorists and pedestrians can read it. This is the hottest trend in protests at the moment and a favorite among photojournalists for news coverage. Bad aspects of banner droppings? A banner is cumbersome and expensive to make. And if the letters are too small, no one will be able to read it as they drive or walk by. Custom-made banners are best. To order one from a company, look under "Signs" in the Yellow Pages.

CDs. No, not compact discs—or, if you're financially literate, "certificates of deposit." CD is short for civil disobedience. The idea was most famously espoused by Henry David Thoreau, a philosopher and author who believed that "there will never be a really free and enlightened State until the State comes to recognize the individual as a higher and independent power, from which all its own power and authority are derived, and treats him accordingly." In simple English, when there are acts of oppression occurring, some activists will risk arrest to fight the higher power in an attempt to end that oppression. Civil disobedience is a very personal act of protest that should not be taken lightly. I have never attempted CD and recommend novice activists take the same route. To learn more about CD, write to YouthPeace at 339 Lafayette Street, New York, NY 10012, or call 800-WRL-YOUTH and request a copy of their *Handbook for Nonviolent Action.*

ELECTRONIC PROTESTS. Some of the country's best protest organizers bring thousands of people together from the comfort of their own living rooms. How? With more people going "on-line," Internet postings are becoming a popular form of protest. Cyberspace is becoming a place to organize, strategize, and rally people who are working on the same issues. It is cheaper than a phone call and faster than the postal service. Computer-literate activists can send information through e-mail, list-servers, and electronic newsletters. This is very popular among college students who often have free Internet access at school. The downside of electronic protests: If you don't own a computer, what good do they do you?

TIP: For information about creating your own activist Web site, go on-line and check out the Activist's Web Starter Kit: http://www2.portal.ca/~comprev/webkit/webkit.htm

RALLIES. Instead of dropping banners, wearing funny-looking costumes, or blocking entrances to office buildings, many people choose to protest through rallies. Usually done with large numbers of people—sometimes as high as five thousand people in one auditorium—rallies are terrific opportunities to energize people into taking action against a specific corporation or abuse. The media will be more sympathetic to a rally than to other types of protest because you chose to avoid confrontation with opposing forces. The problem with rallies? If you don't have large numbers of people attending—one hundred minimum—the media will be quick to call your event a flop.

With such a wide selection of protests to choose from, you're sure to find the right one for the right cause.

FUR THINGS, FIRST

Case situation: Your campaign to stop a retailer's plan to sell fur coats is getting nowhere. You've inspired hundreds of people to write letters to the company; you've convinced hundreds more to boycott the stores; and still, six months later, the company refuses to drop its plans. You decide to organize a protest outside one of its "68 centrally located stores" and make your message heard loud and clear.

What follows are some basic tools and resources I use for protest organizing. Each town is different (e.g., some require permits, while others do not), so always custom-tailor your protest to the community's requirements. Some things to consider when planning a protest:

Permits

Contact your town's public works department and ask about their public gathering requirements. If you need to apply for a permit, do it! That way, the police department will be notified of your protest and will help keep partici-pants and bystanders on their best behavior. You may be required to pay a processing fee, but if it's more than $10, challenge it. Expensive fees are unnecessary and might be waived if you complain enough.

If the town does not require a permit, you should still notify the police. Despite what some people may think about our men and women in blue, they *are* here to protect us. By contacting the police department, you'll be pro-tected against any repercussions from the opposing side.

If your town does not require a permit, get them to put it in writing. You can present it as evidence to any demanding policemen during the protest.

Media

Contact the media using the skills in Chapter 3. If your protest starts at 1:00 P.M. notify the media that it starts at

ISN'T IT IRONIC, DON'T YOU THINK?

In November 1994, when I organized a demonstration outside a fur store in my hometown of Reading, Pennsylvania, it seemed like just another routine protest. I had done everything to make sure it went smoothly: cleared permission from the city, notified the police department ahead of time, and brought ample signs and water for the protesters. So what could go wrong?

As we gathered outside of 127 North Fifth Street holding our "Fur Is Dead" signs, hundreds of people cheered in support of our protest. But the store's owner would have none of it: He screamed to us that he had notified the police and mentioned he would get preferential treatment for being a "considerable" taxpayer in the city. As if. Then I showed him the permission letter from City Hall allowing us to have a public gathering outside his store and even provided him with a copy. Something must've been in the air that day, because what happened next will surely remain on my top-ten list of activist stories.

He punched me. It wasn't a hard hit, and under normal circumstances I wouldn't think twice about the childish action. But the fact he would attempt to do something even remotely violent in broad daylight in front of dozens of people angered me. I, fortunately, didn't strike back, because (a) I knew I could file assault charges when the police arrived, and (b) I couldn't—after he hit me, he ran back into the store and locked the door behind him. A monetary fine and a perhaps a few hours in jail would teach this guy a lesson or two about proper protest etiquette.

Because of all the commotion the store owner caused, more than a dozen police cars (including a paddy wagon, of all things) arrived at the scene of the crime in record time. No one was arrested, even though I insisted on pressing charges against my assailant. But I didn't care. Because the police had blocked the only street from which the fur store was accessible, not one customer could make his or her way to buy fur that day. And since my goal for the protest was to discourage people from patronizing the store, my protest was a success. Learn from my lesson and always notify the men and women in blue about your protests; they might be more help than you think.

1:15 P.M. The extra fifteen minutes gives late protesters time to arrive.

Ask like-minded national organizations (like PETA, if you're an animal rights group) to send a media advisory about your protest to their list of journalists in your area. You can never send out too many news releases.

TIP: Never tailor your protest to fit the media's needs. If a camera crew asks you to do anything out of the ordinary to make their story more interesting, tell them no. Journalists are there to cover news, not create it. For example, a television news station once asked me to start chanting at a protest for their six o'clock broadcast. I turned them down and explained the ethics of journalism to them.

Art Supplies

Buy several jars of red, blue, and green acrylic paint (they show up best on the street and on TV). Use them to paint signs and banners.

Purchase large markers with a fat tip no less than 1/2-inch thick. Fat markers speed up the time it takes to write out words on posters.

Buy a large roll of kraft paper. Brown kraft paper is an economical, ecologically sound alternative to plastic vinyl banners. Use large sheets to make last-minute banners for unexpected protesters. Be sure to recycle the banners when finished!

Purchase large quantities of white, or if you can splurge, color poster board from a warehouse club or office supply store. Look for sales to get the best price.

TIP: Look for ways to receive art supplies as an "in-kind" donation from a school, art supply store, or your workplace. Supplies can be expensive; the more you can get free, the more money you save.

Clothing

All too often, people do not dress for the weather. Either hot or cold weather tends to be more noticeable during a protest for a simple reason: You're just standing there. If the weather is cold, prepare for the harsh conditions by layering your clothing. This has two benefits: You can take layers off if you're too warm, and you can offer that extra scarf or shirt to a person who's dressed too lightly. If the weatherman calls for hot weather, wear light-colored clothing and a hat. Don't forget to bring sunscreen to protect yourself from sunburn.

If you think it is appropriate, urge protesters to wear conservative clothing. Doing so will give your group more credibility by refuting the "radical hippie" stereotype.

A word to animal rights activists: Be sure your message of compassion for animals agrees with your clothing choices. People driving by will pay close attention to your footwear. Don't wear leather; your convictions should be true from head to toe.

Food and Drink

For warm weather, purchase a case of bottled water and freeze it the night before the protest. The next day, people will have an ample supply of cold water.

For cold weather, brew large batches of herbal tea or coffee and store them in thermal containers. Hot drinks will keep people warm and happy.

Don't bring food. Food, I've discovered, encourages people to socialize. Leave the finger sandwiches and brownies at home!

Slogans

Create slogans that are short and sweet. An antifur protest might use "Fur Is Dead" on individual signs and "Get a feel for fur: Slam your fingers in a car door" for its banner.

Short slogans for signs; longer, creative phrases for banners. Let your imagination run free!

GETTING PEOPLE THERE

The hardest part in protest organizing is convincing enough people to show up. Sometimes even the best activists can't come because of work, family, or other commitments. Some people are also just not interested in standing out in the hot sun for an hour. To get people to attend your protest, try to make it more appealing. Try these:

INVITATIONS. Ever notice how some people go out of their way to go to a party? People like to be invited to things; it makes them feel special. Mail "invitations" at least three weeks in advance inviting people to attend your protest. Provide all the information they need to know: Where and when the protest is happening; who is organizing the protest; and why they need to protest. Ask them to RSVP as soon as possible.

PARTY AFTERWARD. I admit it! I've protested just to attend a free party when the demonstration was over. In your invitation, mention there'll be a party to celebrate the day's success. Free food and drink equals free fun to a lot of people.

HAVE THE PROTEST ON A WEEKEND OR HOLIDAY. Most people work during the week and cannot take time off to attend a protest. If you plan your event on a weekend or holiday, when most people have free time, your chances of getting a good number of people to show up are higher. Holidays to avoid: Christmas, Thanksgiving, and Easter.

INVITE THE PUBLIC. If your protest/rally is on something most people can agree with (e.g., fighting a specific disease), encourage people to attend your event via the media. Either send your news release to the local newspaper or pay for a print ad to run two weeks prior to the event. Don't do this if your topic is even remotely controversial, like abortion rights. You risk encouraging the other side to organize a counterprotest.

AFTER THE PROTEST

When all of the chanting and sign holding is finished, there are a few things you should do.

LEAVE THE PROTEST SITE SPOTLESS. If you fail to pick up your trash, including signs and water bottles, you risk getting a fine for littering.

THANK EVERYONE. Be sure to thank the protesters, the reporters, and even the police for helping out. This is a show of courtesy that will be remembered at future protests. The more allies you can win the better.

NEWS CLIPPINGS. Make photocopies of any news clippings about the protest. Fax a copy to the main office of the protested business. Doing so may sway them to concede to your demands. Nobody likes bad PR.

A FEW WORDS

Phew! Who would've thought protests were so complex? But when done right, a protest can be a great way to bring people together. It educates the public about your issue while at the same time telling an opposing force to sit up and listen. Organizing a good protest takes a lot of time and patience, but the results of your hard work are worth it.

TOOLS OF THE TRADE

• Contact the Center for Campus Organizing (CCO) and order a copy of their *Campus Organizing Guide for Peace and Justice Groups*. This guide has tips and advice for organizing events and demonstrations. Send a check for $2.50, payable to "Center for Campus Organizing," to: CCO, P.O. Box 748, Cambridge, MA 02142.

• Read *The Right to Protest* by the American Civil Liberties Union (Carbondale: Southern Illinois University Press, 1991). It gives a synopsis of your rights to free expression through protest activities.

Chapter Nine

The Single Guy

I know. To many of you, the thought of starting a new organization from scratch is too much work. After all, you can't drop school, work, and family just to save the planet. Don't worry. You can still make a significant impact on your community by becoming a one-person army. With a little imagination and time, you'll be able to become an effective advocate by maximizing your available resources and skills. You can make a difference all by yourself.

I learned just how much one person could do when I was only thirteen years old. It was fall, and my friend Sue and I stood in my childhood haunt I called Hidden Pond. Hidden Pond was located in Green Hills, a tiny Pennsylvania community. It was a sixty-six-acre forest comprising rolling hills, a mix of coniferous and deciduous trees, and wildflowers (including fields of orchids) with a good-size pond tucked away in the middle. The area belonged to an elderly woman who used it as a summer campsite where she, according to rumors, would sit in her canoe in the middle of the pond and shoot water snakes. As we looked at the trees around us, Sue turned to me and asked, "Why do the leaves change color?" I responded to Sue's question with "They just do," and proceeded to run through a shallow creek. She followed and fell flat on her face into the murky water.

Sue demanded we leave so she could clean up. I followed her, who looked like a swamp monster from a B movie, up a steep trail to her home and saw something I hadn't noticed before. A giant sign towered over the entrance of Hidden Pond. It announced that our playground was to become another housing subdivision for people to, as the sign put it, "get back to nature." Sue, who was covered in mud and dead leaves, began to cry on my shoulder and whispered, "We have to do something to save Hidden Pond!" I couldn't have agreed more and came up with a plan. First, Sue would have to shower. Second, I would save Hidden Pond.

As a thirteen-year-old, I could have been described as naive. I believed all people were good people. I believed if I met with the developers and asked them to cancel the Hidden Pond project, they would.

The next morning, I walked right up to the office receptionist and said, "Hi! I'm Danny Seo and I want to talk to the people who want to destroy Hidden Pond." I thought to myself, Why beat about the bush? I presented my case, arguing that the forest already had hundreds of homes: squirrel villas, deer condos, and bird tree houses. To this day, I have not forgotten their response: "The animals can just go somewhere else. Anyway, you're just a kid; what do you know?" Unable to respond, I was escorted out by a team of security guards.

I walked around Hidden Pond for several hours looking for an answer to my dilemma. When all seemed hopeless, I tripped over a large piece of pottery sticking out of the ground. Having spent two weeks studying local archaeology, I knew I had uncovered the way to save Hidden Pond. Eagerly, I dug glass bottles, earthenware plates, rusted hinges, and large clay crocks out of the earth. These artifacts, which I stuffed into my pants and jacket pockets, would be key in my plans to have Hidden Pond named a historic site, therefore stopping the development plans.

I had the pieces studied by a team of archaeology instructors. They confirmed that the artifacts were indeed pieces of historic significance dating back to the early nineteenth century. Armed with these new groundbreaking findings, I wrote a letter to a reporter at my local newspaper and convinced him to write several articles about the campaign. It was, after all, a hot story; it's not every day a teenager decides to battle a multimillion-dollar development corporation.

I strongly believe the media is a powerful vehicle for change. With headlines screaming "Teen Battles Developer" and "Teenager's Interest Is Admirable," I recruited hundreds of people into my campaign. These articles powered the Save Hidden Pond campaign.

A prominent environmental attorney donated her services on a pro-bono basis (no fee). She made phone calls to the developer's attorneys and to dozens of high-ranking elected officials. I met with those officials and successfully lobbied them to join the campaign; many wrote endorsement letters urging that Hidden Pond be preserved. Some even made a personal financial contribution to my cause.

And I continued to saturate the media with my preservation message. I wrote more letters to the editor, faxed out dozens of news releases, and appeared on regional nightly news shows. Soon I was known as "the forest kid" by an overwhelmingly supportive community.

And I campaigned nonstop in other ways, too. I designed colorful flyers and distributed thousands around town. Friends painted hundreds of handmade posters and hung them in stores, on bulletin boards, and even on the "Lots for Sale" sign outside Hidden Pond. The artifacts were exhibited at local shopping malls to spur public interest. I even went door-to-door late at night sharing my story one person at a time.

But even with the growing support and my perseverance, I couldn't match the money and the powerful legal team the developers had. I was barraged with threats of potential lawsuits from their lawyers via certified mail both at home and at school. I was barred from ever going near Hidden Pond or legal action would be taken against me. And even my brilliant attorney had delivered bad news to me: She was leaving town because of family matters.

I didn't save Hidden Pond. Today, a long macadam road stretches through the middle of the forest and a few families claim residency in what used to be my playground. But my campaign became a symbol for what people can do when they stand up together to fight for what is right. Because even though I lost the battle to save Hidden Pond, I succeeded in another way: The development corporation I had fought so hard against decided this would be their last attempt to develop a forest. The Hidden Pond development project was an economic disaster for them. They learned their lesson. And that is one victory I can be proud of.

I still receive letters from people all over the country who read accounts of this historic campaign. Most are from adults who praise my "amazing ability to do so much at such a young age," while others are critical of my disrespect for the "developer's property rights." And I enjoy these letters. But the best letter I've ever received simply stated, "Thank you for caring about Hidden Pond."

But you don't have to mobilize a whole town to make a difference. On the contrary, there are lots of other ways to express your views and change the world.

WORKING THE MEDIA

Even without an organization behind you, you can get your opinion heard. The best way to start is with the three media outlets: television, radio, and print. You won't be writing news releases or creating press kits in your one-person campaign. Instead, you'll be commenting on erroneous stories or features, and in the process keeping out-of-line journalists and producers in line with your views.

NEWSPAPERS. Write a "Letter to the Editor" four times a year. If you disagree with an editorial or news article written in the newspaper, let the editor and readership know about it. Writing a letter to the editor is easy. Letters should be brief (two hundred words) and address a specific topic of general public concern or interest. For verification purposes, include your full name, address, and telephone number. Concise letters will get preferential treatment. Check your newspaper for specific guidelines and an address to send your letter to.

If you have good writing skills, contact the editor of a small newspaper and offer to write a weekly, biweekly, or monthly column for their publication *free of charge*. Small newspapers are usually struggling financially, so your offer to write for them gratis might be eagerly accepted. Who knows? Maybe your free writing will turn into a full-time, salaried job by the end of the year. Give it a try.

MAGAZINES. Reach a national audience by sending a letter to your favorite magazine. If you disagree with comments made in the magazine, send a letter explaining why you oppose those views. Or, if you agree with a controversial article, send a letter of support for that point of view.

TELEVISION. Contact national television networks when a show does or promotes something you deem offensive. Send your letter to "The Office of the President." For example, if you believe a kids' show is too violent, write to the network and express your feelings about it. Write to: ABC, 1330 Avenue of the Americas, New York, NY 10019; CBS, 51 West 52nd Street, New York, NY 10019; NBC, 30 Rockefeller Plaza, New York, NY 10020; FOX, 10201 West Pico, Los Angeles, CA 90035; PBS, 1320 Braddock Place, Alexandria, VA 22314-1698. For cable networks, check your *TV Times* circular, found in most Sunday newspapers.

RADIO. Call a radio talk show to confront opposing views or support like-minded guests. Let the listening audience know where you stand.

POLLS. Participate in polls offered by your local newspaper or television nightly news show. Surprisingly, many legislators check these polls to get a general feel as to how their constituents feel about certain issues. A legislator in my county voted against a bill outlawing pigeon shoots because the poll in my paper indicated most people in his district supported shooting pigeons. (Ironically, "Hard Copy"'s poll indicated 99 percent of Americans oppose the shoots. Hmmm . . .)

TAKING FINANCIAL STOCK

The way you handle your financial transactions and investments can have a profound impact on our world. By purchasing affinity checks, using affinity credit cards, and investing in socially responsible mutual funds, you can support various advocacy groups without even trying. Check out these resources:

CONSCIENCE CHECKS. Order specialty checks that benefit your favorite organization instead of buying checks from the bank. These checks support the work of organizations like the Sierra Club, Greenpeace, and the National Organization for Women. For free information, contact Message! Products toll-free at 800-243-2565 or write them at: P.O. Box 64800, St. Paul, MN 55164-0800 or visit their Web site: http://www.greenmoney.com/message

SOCIALLY RESPONSIBLE INVESTING. Choose a mutual fund that invests not only in profitable businesses but also in businesses promoting positive social change. Here are some sample firms (not necessarily an endorsement):

Calvert Group. Founded in 1982, Calvert Group is the creator of the first environmentally and socially responsible funds. Call 800-368-2748 for a free prospectus or visit their Web site: http://www.calvertgroup.com

Pax World Fund. This is a no-load, diversified mutual fund that invests only in industries involved with pollution control, health care, and education. They do not invest in weapons, tobacco, alcohol, or gambling industries. Call 800-767-1729 for a free prospectus or write: 224 State Street, Portsmouth, NH 03801.

For general information about socially responsible investing, contact *The Greenmoney Journal*, a newsletter covering the latest in socially responsible investing and business. Write: West 608 Glass Avenue, Spokane, WA, 99205; or check out their Web site: http://www.greenmoney.com

TIP: When choosing a fund, make sure the person managing your money is not just socially responsible but also a whiz at picking stocks.

PLASTIC WITH PURPOSE. Every time you use an affinity credit card, a portion of your purchase (around ten cents) goes to support nonprofit groups like Planned Parenthood, Family Violence Prevention Fund, and Handgun Control. For free information about their affinity Master-Card and Visa contact Working Assets at 800-788-8588, or, if possible, sign up for a card from your favorite national organization.

TIP: Be sure you sign up for a card that guarantees a donation will be made to a specific charity. Many credit cards look like they support a charity but really don't. For example, a credit card with a picture of a forest on it does not necessarily give any funds to an environmental group. Do your homework.

BUY RIGHT. Instead of hitting the mall during the holiday season, purchase from catalogs and stores run by nonprofit organizations. Purchase calendars, T-shirts, coffee mugs, books, and other items that benefit a worthy charity. A portion of each sale will go directly to support the designated group's work.

CONSUMER ACTIVISM

Let corporations, retail business, and industry know how you feel about their goods or services. Very few people ever take the time to express their feelings to a corporation, so your comments could play a critical role in the way a corporation does business.

CALL 800 NUMBERS. Call a corporation's toll-free hot line to protest an unethical action they may have taken. A few years ago, consumers flooded the 800 comment lines of Starkist, makers of Starkist tuna, to protest the killing of dolphins in tuna drift nets. The company feared economic disaster from this public relations nightmare, so they quickly announced they would only use "dolphin-safe" tuna. Your call could convince other companies to change their ways.

PETITIONS. Circulate a copy of a petition (e.g., a pledge to boycott a corporation) from your favorite national organization. You can get copies through the publications department or campaigns office. Either pass it among coworkers or post it on a bulletin board for people to sign. When completely filled, fax it to the boycotted corporation and send the original via the mail.

TEAR IT UP. Send your cut-up store credit card to the chairman of a retail corporation to protest an action the corporation took. Include a letter explaining why you are returning the card. Your one credit card has an incredible impact and will be felt by the chief decision makers at the company.

Keep your eyes and ears open to stories of corporate abuse. When you object to a corporation's policy or business practices, comment. Your opinions will only count when they hear how you feel. Speak up!

ARMCHAIR LOBBYING

Don't have time to meet with your legislators? Not a problem. Don't even have time to write a personal letter to your legislator? Not a problem. For activists looking for ways to save time, try armchair lobbying.

Purchase one hundred postage-paid postcards from the post office. It'll cost you $20. Now, at a moment's notice, you can send a quick letter of protest or support on pending federal legislation to your legislators. Send a postcard when reading a story about congressional efforts in the morning newspaper. Or send one when a congressional report on the six o'clock news outrages you. Either way, you'll always be ready. Here are some important addresses:

The White House, 1600 Pennsylvania Avenue, NW, Washington, DC 20516

Senator _____, U.S. Senate, Washington, DC 20510

Representative _____, U.S. House of Representatives, Washington, DC 20515

TIP: You can find out the names of your federal representative and two federal senators by contacting your local League of Women Voters. Also, the League can give you the names and addresses of your local and state elected officials. Check the blue pages in your phone book for your town's local LWV chapter.

JOIN 20/20 VISION. This is an organization of national and local policy experts who pinpoint the most timely and important environmental and peace issues facing your community, state, and region. Members receive a monthly postcard detailing a twenty-minute strategic action they can take. The August 1996 postcard urged subscribers to write their congresspeople to support the federal Act to Save America's Forests bill. And every six months, 20/20 Vision sends you a follow-up report on the results of its members' efforts. Contact 20/20 Vision at: 1828 Jefferson Place, NW, Washington, DC 20036; or call 800-669-1782 for a membership form.

JOIN A NATIONAL ORGANIZATION'S ACTIVIST NETWORK. Many groups, including the National Rifle Association, the Humane Society of the United States, and the Human Rights Campaign Fund, have such programs. A network alerts its active members to pending legislation at all levels of government that needs letters of support or opposition. It's armchair lobbying made easy.

SWITCH PHONE CARRIERS. Working Assets Long-Distance Service gives a percentage of your monthly phone bill to groups like Planned Parenthood and the National Minority AIDS Council. But they also update you on key legislative bills in Congress on your monthly phone statement. They even foot the bill for your call to Washington. For information, call 800-788-8588 or visit their Web site: http://www.wald.com

ATTEND A HEARING. Contact your state legislator to obtain permission to attend a legislative hearing at your state capitol. See government in action and learn a few things about civics. You'll be surprised how interesting the hearings are. Bring a friend.

VOTE. Your vote counts at all levels of government. It's your responsibility, not your right, to vote. To register to vote, call 800-249-VOTE or check out Rock the Vote's Web site: http://www.rockthevote.org

SUPPOSE YOU HAD $20

Instead of spending twenty bucks to buy a pair of "slightly damaged" denim jeans from the Gap, use it to do good. By using your money to help a nonprofit group, enlighten a young mind, or educate an elected official, you're making a bigger impact than you might think. Here are some ways to spend a few dollars to do just that:

DONATE A SUBSCRIPTION. Pick your favorite topic-oriented magazine (e.g., *Audubon* for conservation) and donate a year's subscription to the local public or high school library.

BUY BULK BOOKS. Purchase a few copies of your favorite topic-oriented book and send one each to your state representative and senator. Your book will educate them about your interests and, in essence, lobby them on future legislation. And yes, I will make a plug for my own book: Purchase copies of this book and distribute them to local high school libraries to teach a young person how to make a difference.

DISTRIBUTE VIDEOS. Many national organizations sell professionally produced videos about their work and campaigns. Order copies of your favorites and give them to public libraries and video stores for their community-service section. The public can rent these movies free of charge.

RENEW YOUR MEMBERSHIP. National organizations depend heavily on membership dues for income; to some groups, dues represent 90 percent of their funding. Be sure to pay your basic dues every year. If you're worried about receiving annoying mailings throughout the year, request that your name not be brokered to other organizations or businesses. Another reason to renew: If your favorite organization is a 501(c)3 organization, your contribution is tax deductible.

GIFT MEMBERSHIPS. Buy your friend or legislator a year's membership in your favorite national group. They'll receive the publications and materials year-round, keeping them informed of issues you care about. Remember to make clear on the membership form the individual who is receiving the new membership and that you're the one paying the dues.

ON A SPARE SATURDAY MORNING

No matter how busy you think your life is, you will have a spare weekday or weekend to devote some time to a project. If Martha Stewart has time to make potpourri sachets, you have time for an advocacy project. Here are several small projects that are easy to accomplish and can make a dramatic impact on your cause. Try one on your free day.

MAKE A LIBRARY DISPLAY. Ask the librarian at your local public library for permission to set up a display about your issue. For example, if your main issue of concern is abortion rights, you can create a display using pamphlets, facts, and charts from Planned Parenthood, as well as a listing of local support groups.

MAKE A VERTICAL FILE. Gather news clippings, photographs, pamphlets, charts, graphs, and posters about your cause for a special vertical file for your library. These files cover general topics from homelessness to AIDS prevention and are used by students for research projects. Be sure to ask the librarian for permission first.

GET A POLITICAL LIFE. Help out a candidate you support by volunteering for his or her campaign. On a weekend morning, your duties may include posting signs around town, working the phones, or stuffing envelopes for a mass mailing. Your help will make a big difference in their campaign. Contact the local Democratic or Republican Committee in your town for information on how you can help.

THANK SOMEONE. Write several thank-you letters to legislators or corporations for doing the right thing. Rarely do they receive kind letters for doing good deeds. Your doing so will encourage them to continue their streak of goodness.

VOLUNTEER. Spend a few hours helping out at a local community nonprofit center. Walk the dogs at the animal shelter. Help cook lunch at the church soup kitchen. Create a database program for a local AIDS hospice. Do your part.

WHAT YOU CAN DO IN ONE MINUTE

That busy, huh? There are several small things you can do to express your opinions, and they all take less than one minute. Don't disappoint me by making these actions the only things you'll do for our planet; add them to other ideas and skills addressed in the book.

WEAR A PIN. Purchase a lapel pin that has your favorite political slogan on it, like "Save the Whales," "Newt-er Gingrich," or "Equal Rights Now!" Everyone—your friends, family, and coworkers—will know where you stand on the issues.

BUMPER STICKERS. Put a bumper sticker on your car. Popular stickers spotted in my hometown (and yes, I disagree with all of them) include: "Abortion Is NOT Health Care," "I Am the NRA," and "Dole/Kemp '96."

SPORT A T-SHIRT. Wear a T-shirt with your favorite political or social slogan on it, like "Save America's Forests" or "National Health Care Now!"

Naturally, you can't do everything listed in this book or even this chapter. If you did, you would burn yourself out. Choose a few ideas that interest you and try to incorporate them into your daily routine. For example, every morning while you're making coffee, fill out a postcard to the president and mail it. Or while you're getting dressed to go shopping, add a pin to your wardrobe. Every action you take, big and small, makes a difference.

TOOLS OF THE TRADE

Sign up to receive a free subscription to *Build*, the quarterly magazine of Do Something. Keep yourself up-to-date on the latest activism ideas, trends, and resources. For a free subscription, send your name and address requesting "Free Subscription to *Build*," to: Do Something, c/o Subscription Department, 423 West 55th Street, 8th Floor, New York, NY 10019.

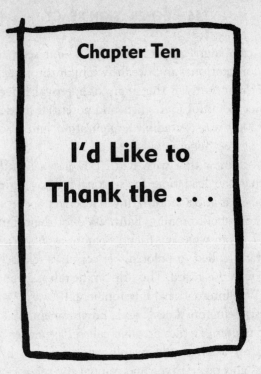

Chapter Ten

I'd Like to Thank the . . .

Movie stars have Oscars, stage actors have Tonys, and musicians have Grammys to recognize outstanding achievement. In the world of community service, there are also awards—big and small—and they, too, bring prestige, prominence, and credibility to activists and their organizations. These awards can be the key to making an organization succeed beyond its wildest dreams.

In 1994, after returning from a weekend trip to Connecticut to accept the Albert Schweitzer environmental award, I realized the benefits of being an award recipient went farther than the shiny plaque, $500 prize, and vegetarian lunch. The award could help me launch unique media campaigns about Earth 2000 and seek funding from corporations and wealthy philanthropists. I believed the award was the stamp of approval I needed to convince doubtful journalists and potential funders that Earth 2000 was a credible organization and not just a bunch of tree-hugging kids.

I also knew that with Earth Day just a month away (and that the lead time for seasonal/holiday articles for newspapers is also a month), it was a perfect opportunity to ask editors about profiling Earth 2000 for their Earth Day issues. I wrote what my friend Sharon, a public relations consultant, called "a tailored, perfect news release" about having won the award. The title on the release read "Local Teens Win International Environmental Award," with the emphasis being on "Local" and "Environmental." I used a new computer graphics program called Pagemaker 3.0 and created an aesthetically pleasing news release by using graphics and reverse type and printed the release on 100-percent recycled paper.

I also wrote a personal letter to each journalist and editor receiving the release. It was a pitch letter, giving reason after reason why Earth 2000 was the only organization right for a feature and why their respective newspapers should devote two full pages to my organization. Sharon told me that if I were selling vacuums, the editors would've surely bought one. That was the only approval I needed to send out the press kits with confidence.

A few days later, my hometown newspaper, the *Reading Eagle/Times*, contacted me about featuring Earth 2000 in their Lifestyle section. I was a bit surprised; not at their positive response but at their suggestion of putting our story in the Lifestyle section, next to sewing tips, Ann Landers, and wedding announcements. I wanted our story in the hard news section, next to stories about war-torn Bosnia and the president's new tax-relief plan. But, following the simple public relations rule that "all publicity is good publicity," I accepted their offer.

On April 22, when the article appeared, the newspaper proclaimed me the "Green Teen" because my birthday is on Earth Day. ("It's a sign!" many have said.) I was forced to face my classmates as, throughout the day, they read from the article, sarcastically repeating my quotes. Just about everyone I met that day said, "Hey! Aren't you the Green Teen?" Need I say more?

Despite the jokes, the article did give Earth 2000 the needed credibility to get funds from a handful of corporations and philanthropists. And because the newspaper devoted two full pages to the article (an unusual decision, since most newspapers are usually pressed for space), it was hard for the more than 100,000 *Reading Eagle/Times* subscribers to miss it. Many even sent checks to support Earth 2000. Today, I still use the article for personal public relations work.

Whether you use the awards to gain media attention or to win the support of potential funders, you should remember, as I do, to be innovative. An award is not just a prime photo opportunity, it is another way to help make your group the best it can be.

AND THE WINNER IS . . .

Awards, in general, range from local community awards that offer no financial incentive to competitive national awards with prizes as high as $1 million. Here's an eclectic

pick of a few national awards and their prizes (not necessarily awards for activism):

Pillsbury Bake-Off Grand Prize	$1 million
Nobel Peace Prize	$930,000
Playmate of the Year	$100,000 plus a Chrysler Eagle Talon in the winner's choice of color
Goldman Environmental Prize	$75,000
Pulitzer Prize	$3,000

Over the past few years, awarding people who "do
good" has become an increasingly prestigious trend. Just
recently, Do Something, a national organization founded
by "Melrose Place" actor Andrew Shue, awarded $10,000
grants to ten people under the age of thirty who are working
to improve their communities. On top of that, one winner
received a $100,000 grand prize bonus. The 125 losing
nominees didn't go away empty-handed; they each got a
$500 consolation prize. Amazing. With big-name sponsors
like MTV, *Mademoiselle*, Blockbuster, Guess?, and America
Online, Do Something was able to distribute more than
$200,000 in prizes for people who do good.

But that's not all. On September 19, 1996, Do Something threw a party in New York City to honor the ten winners. The chairpeople for the event made an impressive list:
Cindy Crawford, Sheryl Crow, George Stephanopoulos,
Michael Stipe, Todd Oldham, Paula Abdul, dozens of
supermodels, and top fashion designers. Tickets sold for as
much as $10,000 a table—*$10,000!* All in the name of
people "doing good."

THE CASE FOR AWARDING GOOD DEEDS

Many experts believe that reliance on external rewards destroys the intrinsic joy of volunteerism. Rewards may be useful to increase productivity and creativity in the short term, but they can also decrease overall performance in the long run. This is only true, in my opinion, if an activist thrives solely on the notoriety, attention, and fifteen minutes of fame the awards provide.

For those of you with self-esteem, winning an award can boost the integrity and prominence of you and your organization. Awards, when used properly and not for self-serving reasons, can help you get in to see big funders, attract additional media attention, and add credibility to a new organization. When you win an award, you are basically receiving a stamp of approval; a group of strangers—the awards committee—is telling others that you're an effective, competent advocate.

In addition to the attention that awards provide, many also offer financial prizes to winners as well as runner-ups. These range from $100 cash prizes to $100,000 grants to start a new community organization. For ethical reasons, you should always donate the winnings to your organization or another nonprofit group. Never, ever, keep the cash prize unless the awards committee *specifically* requires you to do so. Otherwise, you are setting yourself up for some harsh criticism and backlash from the community.

There are awards for everyone—literally. From those honoring individuals who work to find nonanimal alternatives to animal testing to those awarded to people who have the best community spirit, everyone can win for doing something. In a few contests, especially the obscure ones, you are almost guaranteed to win. These receive so few eligible entries that virtually anyone who enters wins. In a few cases, there are more awards than applicants! I know these awards exist; I have won a few just because I was the *only one* who took the time to complete the application.

HOW DO I FIND OUT ABOUT AWARDS?

Unfortunately, there is no book that identifies awards given for community service. (Believe me. I've looked through hundreds of books that had anything remotely to do with awards and prizes.) You've got to investigate and research a number of sources. To find out which awards are available, try these tips:

READ THE NEWSPAPER EVERY DAY. Check the Community Log, Area Highlights, Campus Notes, and any other section that posts notices of awards. If any award appeals to you, write or call for an application and rules form. College students should also read campus publications for listings.

JOIN LIKE-MINDED NATIONAL ORGANIZATIONS. Many national groups have awards programs honoring outstanding members. For example, the Humane Society of the United States (HSUS) has a program that offers monetary prizes to HSUS members who organize the most creative events for Farm Animals Awareness Week. Almost every national organization has at least one contest. Check the group's newsletter and other publications for notices.

READ MAGAZINES. Be on the lookout for contests in mainstream and topic-oriented magazines. Often mainstream publications place tiny blurbs about national contests in their magazines. Topic-oriented publications usually list contests and award competitions that relate to their magazine. For example, environmentalists should read *E Magazine*, a leading environmental publication, to find out about awards in the field of conservation.

WATCH THE TELEVISION NEWS. Religiously watch the *local* televised nightly news shows to hear announcements of local awards. I discovered my local NBC affiliate organized the Jefferson Awards, honoring local people who are "making their communities a better place to live."

MAKE PERSONAL CONTACTS. Ask community leaders, sympathetic elected officials, and colleagues at national like-minded organizations to send you information about awards. Because they are usually the first people to receive information packets about current award opportunities in their respective fields, they can help you track down eligible award programs. I've won several awards just because a staff member at a national group took the time to send me an application.

A FEW NATIONAL COMMUNITY-SERVICE AWARDS

I admit: It's not easy finding awards. To help you get your feet wet, here are a few national awards that honor community-service projects. Many of these receive hundreds of applications every year for a very limited number of awards, so don't expect an easy win. And if you don't win, the experience alone will help you in future competitions. TIP: If you don't win, send a thank-you letter to the committee and ask them to provide any specific comments about your application. Their suggestions will help you create better applications for future contests.

DO SOMETHING. They award grants to individuals under thirty with creative community-building ideas. National grants are available through the New York office in the amount of $500; regional programs in Newark, New Jersey, Boston, and New York City offer local youth $500 grants and sponsor leadership courses. Also, write for information about their BRICK award, an annual competition with a total of $250,000 in prize monies for community-based projects. Contact: Do Something, 423 West 55th Street, 8th Floor, New York, NY 10019; or call 212-523-1175.

FUND FOR SOCIAL ENTREPRENEURS (FFSE). A project of Youth Service America, the FFSE contest seeks visionary young leaders with bold and effective ideas for national and community-service ventures. Winners receive income stipends of $18,000 (year one) and $10,000 (year two), in addition to a $4,000 seed grant. Contact: Youth Service America, 1101 15th Street, NW, Suite 200, Washington, DC 20005; or call 202-296-2992.

***REACT* TAKE ACTION AWARDS.** Parade Publications' interactive weekly for teens, *React* magazine, seeks five outstanding young people ages twelve to seventeen who have made an "enduring, significant contribution to their school, community, nation, and/or the world." Winners receive a $20,000 prize to be used for college. Nominees should show the activism, compassion, and community service that marks them as future leaders. Contact: *React* Take Action Awards, P.O. Box 4619, Grand Central Station, New York, NY 10163; or check out their Web site: http://www.react.com for more information.

THE INGREDIENTS OF A GOOD NOMINATION KIT

Here's what a good nomination kit should include. Remember, every award is different and has its own special requirements. Be sure to tailor your kit.

COVER LETTER. Type a one-page cover letter that has your name, address, and phone number at the top of the page. Concise letters are best. In the first paragraph, thank them for taking the time to consider your application. (You'd be surprised how many people forget.) Briefly discuss your project and credentials. Conclude with a sentence inviting them to contact you "at their convenience" with any questions. Use the sample on page 154 as a guide.

APPLICATION FORM. Be sure to fill out the application completely. If you don't, you risk being disqualified. If you're not sure how to answer a question, don't leave it blank! Call or write the award contact person and ask.

LETTERS OF RECOMMENDATION. Ask community leaders, elected officials, and nonprofit staffers to write letters of recommendation supporting your application. Be sure to get letters that aren't specifically written for a particular award. In other words, the letters should be addressed "To Whom It May Concern." Such generic letters of recommendation can be photocopied and used for other applications.

NEWS CLIPPINGS. Send no more than three news clippings about your work. If possible, send actual copies of the newspaper or magazine. Be sure to mark the article.

BLACK-AND-WHITE PHOTOGRAPH. Send a black-and-white head shot of yourself. When judges can relate a person's work to a face, it makes it more personable. These photos are more professional than color and the standard for many award competitions. Very few applicants remember to send a photo. TIP: Do not send anything larger than a 5 × 7 photo. Big photos are overpowering and weaken the overall strength of your application.

WRITING SKILLS. If your writing skills aren't up to par, ask someone for help. And by all means, make sure all

September 5, 1997

Jennifer Patterson
Shoot Up!
101 Main Street
New York, NY 10020
(212) 555-1111

Do Something Brick Award Committee
423 West 55th Street
8th Floor
New York, NY 10019

Dear Brick Award Committee:

Enclosed is my official nomination for the Do Something Brick Award on behalf of Shoot Up! Thank you for taking the time to consider my request.

As you can see from the enclosed materials, I believe Shoot Up! best meets what Do Something is looking for in an award recipient: an organization that not only helps at-risk teens but also mobilizes teens to get involved in the effort. Consider our qualifications:

*Shoot up! was founded in early 1997 by two teenagers who wanted to provide other teenagers with an alternative to drugs and alcohol. Instead of shooting up drugs, teens are encouraged to "shoot" basketballs, play volleyball, or do any of the twenty free activities offered in the program. More than 200 New York City teens have signed up for the program since its inception.
*25 students have signed up for drug and alcohol counseling to combat their addictions because of the Shoot Up! program.
*Pilot programs are being started in other NYC schools because of the success of the original Shoot Up! program.

The Do Something Brick Award prize money would be used to expand these programs into other schools. A more detailed plan on how the monies would be used is included in the nomination packet.

There is so much more to the Shoot Up! program. I'd like to tell you more about it, and I hope you'll take a moment to read the enclosed materials. If you should have any questions, please do not hesitate to contact me at your earliest convenience.

Best Regards,

Jennifer Patterson

Jennifer Patterson
Cofounder, Shoot Up!

spelling is accurate. Write your application and have a friend edit it.

SUBMIT YOUR APPLICATION ON TIME. Your application won't count if it doesn't make the deadline. Avoid Federal Express or any other overnight mail service unless your nomination absolutely must arrive the very next day.

USE RECYCLED PAPER. Textured papers look nice and give you a "green" edge—bonus points for being ecologically aware. Don't use colored paper. It's difficult to copy from and makes your application look chintzy.

DON'T SEND ANYTHING SOILED OR EVEN SLIGHTLY DIRTY. It seems obvious, but I've seen hundreds of otherwise brilliant applications not win because the papers were stained with coffee or tea. One person even sent a nomination with dried blood on it. Gross!

HOW TO GET NOTICED

To be noticed in the flood of award applications, you have to stand out. Creating a good nomination kit is like creating a good press kit. Follow this rule at all times: Quality beats quantity. Read that again. Instead of sending a nomination kit with dozens of attachments (fifty news clippings, twenty-five letters of recommendation, etc.), send only the best material; the judges don't have time to weed out all of the unimportant papers. If you send a good-size nomination kit, you might even receive bonus points from the judges. Trust me: quality over quantity.

Your chances of winning an award will improve greatly with these tips. If you apply for several awards at the same time, you'll have an even better chance of winning. Keep trying and never, ever, give up!

WHAT TO DO AFTER WINNING

Sadly, many people don't take advantage of the benefits of being an award-winning activist. As I mentioned earlier in the chapter, an award can bring credibility and attention to your cause and organization. When done right, you can extend the longevity of the award and reap the benefits for several years.

TWO WEEKS BEFORE AN AWARDS CEREMONY

SEND OUT A NEWS RELEASE. Fax, mail, or e-mail a news release to every journalist in your immediate area announcing your win. If the ceremony is out of town, fax a news release to journalists in that town, too. In the release, invite them to cover the awards ceremony, to contact you for interviews, and to create a special feature article about your cause. If you get any coverage, try to get an address printed at the end of the article so interested readers can send donations or questions.

TIP: Be sure to get permission from the award organizers prior to sending anything out.

INVITE POTENTIAL FUNDERS TO THE CEREMONY. Mail invitations to corporations and other potential funders you've been courting for grants. They may jump onto the praise bandwagon and give you a check at the ceremony as a show of support. It's good public relations for them, too.

SEND A THANK-YOU LETTER TO THE AWARDS COMMITTEE. Well, duh! *Well*, people forget. Consider this a friendly reminder to thank those who are making all this possible.

WHAT TO DO AFTER THE AWARDS CEREMONY

COLLECT NEWS CLIPPINGS. Make photocopies of news clippings about the award. Keep them handy for future awards, grant proposals, and funding appeals. Whenever you write to someone important—like a senator or CEO—include a copy of the article. It'll add some credibility to your name and command a faster response.

THANK EVERYONE. Send thank-you letters to anyone who helped you win the award. Thank the English teacher who edited your application, members from your group, people you met at the ceremony, journalists who wrote about you, and anyone else who either helped you on the application or showed up to attend the ceremony.

FOR A LIFETIME OF OPPORTUNITY

RECYCLE THE AWARD INTO AN INTRODUCTION. Ever notice how people introduced as Nobel Laureates garner more respect than just plain, old Bob Smith? In a grassroots effort, the award may be enough to convince local schools and Rotary clubs to invite you to present a speech. In their eyes, it's more prestigious to have an award-winning activist than another special-interest person. Sometimes you may even receive an honorarium for your speaking services. This is a payment for your time and trouble. The honorarium, ranging from $50 to $1,000, should always be donated to your organization.

Mention the award in concluding paragraphs of future news releases. Doing so will add credibility to yourself and the organization. See the sample news release in Chapter 3.

CREATE YOUR OWN AWARD. If you discover there is a need for an award, start one. You don't need a lot of money, just some time and good marketing skills. Use the skills you learned from attending award ceremonies to create your own ideal award. Spread the word through the media to find prospective recipients. By developing your own award program, you not only honor those working on your issue, but you bring additional media attention to the overall cause.

Awards are a powerful tool to help further your cause and organization. But don't fall into the "glory trap" by letting awards dominate your life. When you win an award, you serve as an example to others to become active members of the community, not to be a pretentious, conceited snob. Use awards to advance your cause, not yourself.

Chapter Eleven

Internships

I f you've read this far through the book, way to go! You now have all the basic information you need to be a successful activist. Go change the world! But for those of you who yearn to learn more about activism or are even considering making your cause a full-time career, consider interning with a national organization.

WHAT IS AN INTERNSHIP?

The verb "to intern" means "to shut up closely so that escape is impossible or unlikely." Frightening. But despite the definition, an internship is not a prison sentence. It is a volunteer job; an organization "hires" you to do work usually done by paid employees. Many companies and non-profits bring in interns for one simple reason: They can't afford to employ additional staff. In most cases, you are not paid a penny for your work. So, why work full time for zero pay? Simple: experience and connections.

An internship with your favorite national organization can turn into a full-time position. According to a recent study by Northwestern University, 58 percent of interns are eventually offered jobs with their host employers. *Fifty-eight* percent! Because corporations and nonprofits receive stacks of résumés for a few job openings, they are more likely to hire someone they already know—like an intern. It is worth the investment to work for three months *without pay* for the opportunity to receive a salaried position in the organization of your choice.

I'm so accustomed now to activist know-how that I take my skills and my contacts for granted. Calling celebrities for fund-raisers, pitching cover stories to magazines, and even asking corporate CEOs for $25,000 grants in the name of charity has become easy for me. But I couldn't have transformed myself from a fumbling teenager into a successful political/public relations consultant in just three short years without an internship.

When I accepted my internship with The Fund for Animals in 1993, I thought my job would involve sneaking into forests late at night to deter deer hunters, speaking at big antihunting rallies, and running the office—doing, you know, office stuff. But I soon understood that my dreams of an office full of excitement and round-the-clock adventures would be just that: dreams.

When I joined The Fund for Animals staff, I had already been written about in scientific journals, political magazines, and national newspapers. I naturally believed I would be instrumental in major decision-making meetings. But I came from a small town where any teenager who accomplished anything the least bit interesting would get front-page coverage. Once I got to Washington, D.C., I learned the harsh truth: I was the lowest person on The Fund for Animals staff.

I fetched lunches for staffers in blazing 90-degree weather. I was yelled at for standing too close to fax machines or too far from phones ringing nonstop. And I earned a measly $1.04 an hour. I would've been better off working in a store telling people how fabulous they looked in those smashing Gap jeans.

But as the saying goes, What doesn't kill you can only make you stronger. Many monotonous tasks taught me skills no classroom instructor could, like how to update media data banks, organize a bulk direct-mail fund-raising appeal, change the toner in the photocopier, and work the phones late at night looking for support on dying legislation.

The internship allowed me to make mistakes, too. I jammed fax machines. I disconnected incoming phone calls (including one from the group's president). I even occasionally came into work really late. (Who would've thought the Beltway would be so tangled?) I honestly can say that I learned from my mistakes. I am now a pro on the phone, always punctual, and a whiz with a fax machine (even though it's practically idiot-proof).

I slowly adapted to my internship, and eventually they put me in charge of responding to letters from children. I remember how happy I was to be given a real project, not brainless stuff like sealing envelopes or making photocopies. With a computer in front of me, a stack of amusing letters from children, and a temporary desk to call my very own, I set out to do the best job on my own "very critical" (their words, not mine) project.

The first letter was a blast to read and respond to. The second was amusing. The third was interesting. By the fourth I was getting frustrated and bored. I began to dread responding to the hundreds of letters piled high on my desk. It's not that I didn't love reading sweet, kind, innocent letters from children. But how is it possible to answer questions like "How can I stop hunting?" or "Why did Bambi's mom have to die?" in simple, one-syllable words. And don't think for a minute I could respond with a form letter to each kid's request; they might be upset if they didn't receive a detailed response to their inquiries. Every letter needed the personal touch. It became the never-ending project.

By the end of my internship, I had finished the last letter. This project did teach me something more than just how to relate better with kids—something that was worth its weight in drudgery. It gave me discipline and patience, skills I use today to avoid making sarcastic comments to egotistical executives and rude celebrities.

And tomorrow, when I call Michael Stipe asking him to support a forest preservation group and make an appointment for a haircut so I can look sharp for a Friday meeting with Vice President Al Gore, I'll remember it all started by fetching lunch, making coffee, and writing letters to kids during my internship at The Fund for Animals.

WHAT CAN I EXPECT FROM AN INTERNSHIP?

Every internship is different. If you intern with an organization that mainly lobbies elected officials, you may be expected to coordinate meetings with political staffers and send position papers to senators. If you intern with a nonprofit publication, you may be expected to interview people for articles and spell-check copy for upcoming issues. But every intern can be expected to do clerical work like photocopying and filing at least 25 to 30 percent of the time.

To help you understand the various internships nonprofit organizations offer, here's a selection from a few national ones, including the duties, housing availability, pay (if any), and application requirements. Notice the diversity of each internship program.

CENTER FOR SCIENCE IN THE PUBLIC INTEREST. Interns work in the Washington, D.C., office on nutrition science policy and/or food safety issues. Internships last ten weeks with a $5.25-an-hour wage for undergraduate students. Application process: send cover letter, résumé, writing sample, two letters of recommendation, and official transcript of courses and grades.

CHILDREN'S DEFENSE FUND. Interns provide important staff support by conducting surveys, drafting reports, developing databases, attending congressional hearings, and providing logistical support for workshops and conferences. Interns are not paid and housing is not provided. There are eleven divisions for specialized internships, including the media department and the office of government affairs. Application process: send application, cover letter (serves as writing sample), a résumé, and three references.

FELLOWSHIP OF RECONCILIATION. Interns work in three departments for this national peace and justice organization. Duties include racial and economic justice program coordination, communications/media relations, and local group organizing. Interns receive free housing, medical insurance, and a $600-a-month stipend. Application process: send for application.

***HOW ON EARTH* YOUTH MAGAZINE.** Interns are the backbone of this national publication for "young people's creativity, passion and concern for all life." Housing and food allowance provided. Interns are not paid. Duties include basic office work, magazine editing/layout with added work in the on-site organic gardens. Application process: contact organization for latest internship opportunities.

PEOPLE FOR THE ETHICAL TREATMENT OF ANIMALS. Interns are expected to do administrative and clerical work such as data entry and preparation of mailings. There are $50 stipends available for transportation and food, but limited housing. Application process: send application; a two-page, double-spaced essay; and three letters of recommendation.

LOCATING INTERNSHIPS

First and foremost, you must find out about current internship opportunities. Locating the dream internship is like researching which college or university is right for you. Research, then reject.

• Sit down and make a list of every national organization you would enjoy working for. Then cut the list to six. Call the personnel director of each and ask for information about internship opportunities and an application form.

• Ask contacts at other organizations for information. Staff at those organizations without an internship program can help you locate good ones. They can also warn you about dead-end internships they might've personally experienced. Learn from their mistakes.

• Pick up a current copy of the preferred topic-oriented publication in your field. Check out the classified section for the latest internships being offered by like-minded organizations. Some internships will offer financial incentives in their ads to attract prospective applicants. A list of these publications can be found at the end of this chapter.

• If an organization doesn't have an internship program, offer yourself as one anyway. Some groups are so busy and overworked that such a program has not been launched. You could be the answer to their heavy workload and, in the long run, have a better chance of future employment with the organization.

• After receiving detailed information about internships, discard those that don't interest you. Chances are you'll be unhappy at those places. Also, set aside internships that do not fit within your time frame. For example, if you planned on interning for only one month and a group requires a three-month stay, file that application for future reference.

THE APPLICATION PROCESS

An internship is just like any other job. You need to apply for the position. Your application is the only way the personnel director can get a sense of your personality and qualifications. There is no room for modesty or mistakes in your application. Here are a few tips to make it extraordinary:

BEFORE YOU EVEN START. Make photocopies of the application before you begin to fill it in. People mess up on their applications, so its a good idea to have extra copies just in case. Also, be sure to use a pen when filling out an application.

INCLUDE A RÉSUMÉ. A résumé (a summary of your qualifications and experience) gives the personnel director a quick look at your education, work experience, and special skills. Internship résumés should also include any successful projects you have conceived and completed. Also include any awards you may have received. Even high school students should put together a résumé or, at the least, a list of qualifications. Writing a good résumé takes a lot of practice. Look for books on résumé writing at your local library or check out *How You Really Get Hired* by John L. LaFevre (New York: Prentice Hall 1992).

BE THOROUGH. Be sure to fill out the *entire* application completely. If something doesn't apply to you, write "N/A" to indicate not applicable. Good grammar and punctuation are crucial. And always, *always* check spelling.

ANSWER TRICKY QUESTIONS INTELLIGENTLY. For example, if they ask "What is your worst quality?" reply with a positive quality. "My worst quality is my overeagerness to get a project done as quickly as possible. I just can't relax." A wrong answer would be: "I graduated bottom of my class."

INCLUDE A PHOTOGRAPH OF YOURSELF. Your application will appear more personable to the personnel director when you include a photograph. You don't need a professional photo; a Polaroid will do. Just remember to keep the photo smaller than 5 × 7.

INCLUDE NEWS CLIPPINGS AND LETTERS OF RECOMMENDATION. Send photocopies of the best news clippings and letters of recommendation you have. Doing so will prove your competence and ability to get the job done.

BE A NEAT FREAK. Divide your materials into sections (e.g., news clippings, essay, letters of recommendation) and put them into a new folder. Use clean, unwrinkled paper. Neatness counts big-time.

DON'T LIE. False information will come back to haunt you sooner or later. Start your internship with a clean slate. Don't lie.

DON'T BE CUTE. A friend of mine lost an internship because he wrote down "yes" where the application asked for the sex of the applicant. It may seem funny to you, but it's not amusing to the personnel director. Keep the jokes for your friends.

Internships with national nonprofit groups are easier to obtain than those with a Fortune 500 corporation because very few people bother to apply to nonprofit organizations. So if you follow the preceding tips, you'll be sure to get the internship of your dreams. Now, after you've landed an internship, it's time to . . .

NEGOTIATE YOUR INTERNSHIP

Contrary to popular belief, it is okay to negotiate the terms of your internship after landing one. Nonprofit groups depend heavily on interns to keep their organizations afloat, so you can make some reasonable demands if you decide to accept their internship offer. Before you say yes to any internship, decide what you want to get out of it and ask for it from the start. Here's what you can probably get with enough persistence:

MONEY. Even if they specifically state they do not pay their interns, ask the organization to provide a living stipend for transportation, food, and other living expenses. Start high, around $1,000 a month, and negotiate your way down. But remember, even if you only get $100 a month, that's still better than nothing—most interns receive zero compensation.

HOUSING. If you need a place to live during your internship, and they say they'll provide housing, make sure you have that commitment in writing *before* you move.

A WRITTEN LEARNING AGREEMENT. Ask for a "learning agreement." This is a written contract that outlines what an intern is expected to do and what work experience the intern will receive in return. You will not only impress the personnel director for being so knowledgeable, but you will also protect yourself from getting a dud internship.

REGULAR MEETINGS. Ask to have a weekly meeting with the executive director or supervisor to discuss your progress. Doing so will help keep the line of communication open. These are also good opportunities to pitch new project ideas, introduce innovative ways to streamline the office, and do anything else to impress the head honcho.

FREE WEEKENDS. Many interns are expected to be available at a moment's notice. This is not fair to you. Have your learning agreement state that you will not work on weekends; you deserve to have some time to yourself! Try to get an agreement that states you are not obliged to work more than forty hours a week.

TIP: If you sense your employer is getting disturbed by any of your demands, let them go. But don't accept anything that you feel is totally unfair. The best way to create a fair contract is to have both parties willing to compromise.

REAPING THE INTERN BENEFITS

When everything falls into place, your internship can lead to a great career in your field of interest. Many people who started off as interns are now high-level staff members or even presidents of organizations. But to make sure you do everything right in your transition to an actual salary, follow these tips:

KEEP A JOURNAL. From Day 1 to Day 100 of your internship, keep a log of everything you did. "On August 13, I created an action alert to notify our 50,000 members about a new White House plan to discontinue funding for Head Start." You can use your accomplishments to strengthen your case for full-time employment with either your host employer or with other organizations.

NOTIFY YOUR SUPERVISORS. Three weeks before the end of your internship, notify your supervisor that you will be searching for a salaried position in your field. Ask that they consider you for any current or future employment opportunities. If they have no jobs, ask them to recommend you to other like-minded organizations.

ASK FOR AN EVALUATION. A week before leaving your internship, ask your supervisors for an evaluation of your work. Their comments, if positive, will be crucial in finding employment with other organizations.

SEND A THANK-YOU NOTE. Thank everyone for the opportunity to work with them. Your courtesy will keep your work fresh in everyone's mind. Also, your attention to detail will increase the possibility of a career at that organization.

THINK OF IT AS A TEST. When interning, remember to think of this opportunity as a test of your intelligence, competence, and creativity. Be part of the inventive process at work and become a team player. If, at the end of your internship, your absence will have an adverse effect on their work, you may have just landed yourself a job.

BUT I DON'T WANT A JOB

Not all interns want to land a full-time job. Many people intern with their favorite organization just for the experience and fun of it. People are excited about working full-time with their favorite group, helping out at the national level. Some people even spend their entire summer vacation interning in an organization's office to do their part. They see it as a rewarding experience and love every minute they're there. Here are some other benefits:

RÉSUMÉ. Adding your internship experience to a résumé can improve future employment chances with any type of business (profit *and* nonprofit). Employers like to see diversified individuals who have strong educational and personal skills.

IMPROVED SKILLS. You can use your skills to create or to improve your own grassroots organization. The ideas and strategies you'll pick up from just one week of interning will be invaluable for future campaign efforts.

CONTACTS. It's easier to contact people at national groups about your own projects after your internship. Because they know you, staffers will be more willing to help you. Friends are more likely to help friends.

FOR THE FUN OF IT. Interning can be a fun, fulfilling experience. From building houses in a Costa Rican rain forest to lobbying legislators in Wisconsin, internships are great opportunities to make a real difference while having a lot of fun.

Interning can lead to a successful career with a nonprofit organization. You won't get rich working for a nonprofit, but you'll reap benefits from knowing you're working full time to ease the exploitation, the agony, and the misery humans and animals face in our world. It will enrich your soul.

TOOLS OF THE TRADE

Here are some guide books on locating internships with your favorite organization:

• The Environmental Careers Organization (ECO) lists environmental internships. Write: 286 Congress Street, 3rd Floor, Boston, MA 02110; or call 617-426-4375.

• *EarthWork*. A listing of hands-on, conservation internships. Published by the Student Conservation Association, P.O. Box 550, Charlestown, NH 03603.

• *The Job Seeker*. Write: Route 2, Box 16, Warrens, WI 54666; or call 608-378-4290.

• Also check out the Princeton Review's annual listing of internships available in the United States. *America's Top Internships* and *The Internship Bible* (New York: Random House) are the best directories available listing internship opportunities with groups ranging from Greenpeace to Amnesty International. All are updated quarterly.

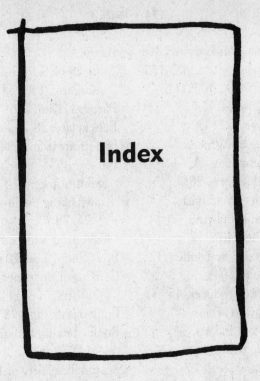

Index

About the Author

Danny Seo, nineteen, is the founder of Earth 2000 National, Inc., a national organization he started with just $10 at age twelve. Under his leadership, Earth 2000 waged ground-breaking campaigns proving young people have the power and will to bring significant, positive advances to the environmental and animal rights movements. From coordinating successful corporate boycott campaigns to launching award-winning educational initiatives, Danny earned the title "America's Most Influential Teen" in 1996 by a leading public relations trade publication.

Danny has appeared in over five hundred media outlets, including *Newsweek, The Wall Street Journal, Family Circle*, and even the tabloid *The National Enquirer*, who dubbed him "out to save more animals than Noah." He is the recipient of numerous awards and accolades, including honors from the Albert Schweitzer Institute for the Humanities and *Who Cares* magazine's 1995 "Young Visionary of the Year."

Danny is a 1995 graduate of Governor Mifflin High School. He frequently travels the United States speaking at national conferences and colleges, and serves as a youth issues, public relations, and fund-raising consultant to political and advocacy organizations. He lives in Washington, D.C. *Generation React* is his first book.

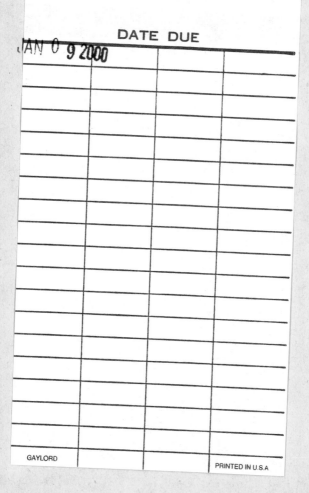

DATE DUE

JAN 0 9 2000			
GAYLORD			PRINTED IN U.S.A